No Glass slipper

No Glass Slipper

✦

Surviving and Conquering Painful Life Experiences

Sharon Coffey, PsyD

iUniverse, Inc.
New York Lincoln Shanghai

No Glass Slipper
Surviving and Conquering Painful Life Experiences

iUniverse books may be ordered through booksellers or by contacting:

iUniverse
2021 Pine Lake Road, Suite 100
Lincoln, NE 68512
www.iuniverse.com
1-800-Authors (1-800-288-4677)

ISBN-13: 978-0-595-38603-1 (pbk)
ISBN-13: 978-0-595-82984-2 (ebk)
ISBN-10: 0-595-38603-2 (pbk)
ISBN-10: 0-595-82984-8 (ebk)

Printed in the United States of America

Dedicated to

My mother,

Frances Coffey Daniels.

A true survivor.

Contents

Introduction xi

CHAPTER 1   Survive! 1

   Meet Challenges Head-on. 2

   Be a Survivor. 2

   Coping with Adversity 3

   Motivation for Those Moments 4

   Lessons Learned 4

CHAPTER 2   Live! 6

   Keep Life Simple. 6

   The Choices Are Yours 7

   Emotions: Can't Live without Them. 7

   Trust Is a Frightening Thing. 8

   Relationships: The Fruit of Life. 10

   Wisdom from the Wise. 10

   No Cinderella 11

CHAPTER 3   The Hansel and Gretel Experience 13

CHAPTER 4   Barbra Streisand: A Queen in Her Glory 17

   When We Were a Family 17

   Mom Needs a Husband 21

   Choosing to Be Different 28

   Oh! The Lights on Broadway 30

   Breaking New Ground 31

   Taught the Hard Way. 32

   And It Feels Good. 33

CHAPTER 5   Lessons from Little Red Riding Hood 34

CHAPTER 6   Oprah Winfrey: Her Highness's Power 38

Hallelujah 38

Will Someone Spare Some Love? 41

Not on My Watch 49

And So I Spoke and They Listened 53

Cruise Control 54

Trial by Fire 56

And So I Was Special 57

CHAPTER 7   Falling with Alice in Wonderland 58

CHAPTER 8   Drew Barrymore: A Popular Princess 62

Baby Girl 62

Sucked In, Sucked Dry 65

School Times 67

Negative Love 68

Drinking and Drugging 69

Who Am I Really? 71

Putting Away the Toys 74

A Hop and a Skip 75

Mom Never Taught Me This 76

It's My Life and I'll Play if I Want To 77

CHAPTER 9   Waking Up with Sleeping Beauty 78

CHAPTER 10   Halle Berry: Royal Beauty 82

Disqualified and Misunderstood 82

Beauty and the Beast 85

Trying Till I Get It Right 92

It's Starting to Click 94

Moving with Caution 96

Reality Testing 97

My Way 98

CHAPTER 11   Enlightenment from The Wizard of Oz 99

CHAPTER 12 Demi Moore: A Duchess's Determination 105

Unvalued Doll 105

Nomadic Chaos 107

Which World Is Mine? 111

A Soapy Start 115

Finding Myself within Myself 116

A Twisty Winding Road 118

Home at Last 119

CHAPTER 13 The Glass Slipper: Cinderella's Lesson 120

CHAPTER 14 Attain and Maintain 124

Hoping We Have It Now 124

Goals 124

Stay Motivated 125

Stay on the Right Path 126

Discouraged? 126

Meet Challenges with Optimism 127

Love Thyself 128

APPENDIX Evaluations and Assessments 129

Survivor Assessment Questionnaire 130

Self-Assessment Questionnaire 131

Main Chapter Highlights 133

Bibliography for individual quotes 135

Bibliography 141

About the Author 151

Introduction

How does a paper cut become an infected wound that could result in the amputation of an arm? The initial "ouch" tells us something is wrong. It may be minor or major at the time it happens, but what we do about it will determine how it heals. Does it grow or does it become a larger wound? Do we treat it or do we ignore it, leaving it open to be further violated? Tending to our wounds is important. We all have them. Some interrupt our lives. Some destroy lives because we allow them to fester and become permanent scars or remain as open wounds. We need to treat our wounds and move on.

The number one reason for low self-esteem and an inability to live a peaceful and productive life is the difficulty we have letting go of painful past experiences. People spend millions of dollars buying self-help books, trying alternative lifestyles, and seeking therapy to rid themselves of the emotional burdens they carry from their past. We judge who we are, how we are valued, and what we can do by our history. It is a common pattern to continue to relive past events, but this prevents us from living our lives fully, putting us into a cycle of never-ending pain.

There are myths that feed the cycle of low self-esteem and self-destructive thoughts. People believe that there is no one who has gone through what they have gone through. As unique as your situation may be, there are others who have had experiences similar to yours. You can learn from them. *No Glass Slipper* presents real-life biographies of women who have gone through extremely traumatic experiences and have been able to move beyond the trauma. Like you, they may have once felt that they didn't have what it takes and could never develop it. But they did, and so can you. In *No Glass Slipper*, you will see the struggles undertaken by these women and learn how they developed what it took to move past their pain.

No one's future has been charted from the past. Your life is what you make of it. The celebrity survivors presented here decided that they would not stay in the adverse conditions into which they had been born. It took some of them longer than others, but each decided that it was time to get off the merry-go-round and move forward.

But they are famous, you might say. Yes, they are, and they've earned it. If you think that people like these had their good lives handed to them or were lucky, your own growth will be hindered by this belief. As the title implies, there are no glass slippers here. These women changed their lives by changing the way they perceived themselves and by staying focused on their goals. Nothing was accomplished through luck, and no one handed them their good fortune. Hard work, both personally and professionally, got them where they are today.

We have the tendency to believe that even if we reach our goals, something awful will happen. Life has taught most of us that good things never last. Not in my world. Roller coasters are a way of life—get on and hold on, and you will be fine. Maintenance is needed to keep what you have, no matter who you are.

No Glass Slipper looks at adverse life conditions as challenges to be conquered, not as debilitating circumstances that will cripple you for life. In perceiving adverse conditions as challenges, you become a survivor instead of a victim. You learn from the difficult times in your life. You look back on them as lessons that had to be learned.

There is a need for individuals to find answers to questions such as, "How can I be better?" or "How can I live better?" The issues are endless, and when these issues are not addressed, people become depressed, sometimes seeking professional therapy and sometimes using therapeutic self-help aids. When people have difficulties in their relationships they seek help in the form of counseling and read self help books or other aids which they feel will give them guidance. When an individual wants to improve themselves they read information which offers them guidance in self improvement and attend workshops geared at becoming a better "you". Most talk shows are successful because besides the entertainment value they have they give their viewers a lesson on how to improve themselves and live a better life.

We live as we believe we are destined to live, not as we desire to live. We view ourselves through perceptions that have been defined by our experiences. We then predict our futures within these limited confines. When things turn out the way we predicted, because we have set ourselves up for such outcomes, we say to ourselves, "See, I knew it all the time. Why did I hope for things to be different?" It's the self-fulfilling prophecy. One believes that things will be a certain way and acts accordingly, making those things happen.

As long as you have a negative view of life and of your destiny, you will be stuck in the rut you have defined for yourself. Remember *you* defined this life. It was not previously charted out for you. Your destiny is defined by your future goals and what you wish out of life. Don't sit around waiting for good things to happen. Make them happen. No one is going to rescue you and slip magical slippers on your feet, propelling you into peace and prosperity, because there is no glass slipper.

1

Survive!

"Character cannot be developed in ease and quiet.
Only through experience of trial and suffering can the soul be strengthened,
ambition inspired, and success achieved."
—Helen Keller

There are times when we think we will never survive a painful experience. Anxiety from such experiences causes us to struggle through life, fearing one day after another. It is important to live through these hard times, to grow emotionally, and to gain insight. Every experience adds a necessary thread to the pattern our life is weaving. It helps us to understand tomorrow what we could not understand today; in doing so, we become survivors.

All of us are survivors. None of us has gone through life without hardship. It is how we handle the hardship that keeps it from growing to the point where they devastate us. The fear and dread of yesteryears do not disappear completely. They hover over us, making it difficult to move on, consciously and unconsciously.

What we experience is a part of us, but it is not all of us. We have choices not only about what we do but who we are. Our choices are many. These choices present themselves as challenges.

Why do some people handle life's challenges better than others? Why is it that some people fall apart with every challenging experience, spending most of their lives putting themselves back together? It would take a psychological encyclopedia to answer these questions. There are as many reasons as there are individuals, and the combinations of life experiences make the possibilities infinite.

When we experience hard times, they seem unbearable. Difficulties seem to attract more difficulties, and the domino effect creates a negative attitude. Negativity is something we all struggle with. It creates fear about what lies ahead.

When the good times come, as they always do, they are accompanied by a positive attitude. This is the attitude that we want to carry into the hard times. It will give us the strength we need to tackle the difficult circumstances and challenges that lie ahead.

Meet Challenges Head-on

Today presents a new challenge, just as tomorrow will. Life gives us one challenge after another. Although challenges throughout our lives may be difficult, they offer opportunities for personal growth. Challenges are to be expected. They motivate us and bring purpose to our lives. They develop maturity.

Our greatest challenge is to look forward with secure anticipation and to trust in what the future holds. We often ponder too much on the darker periods in our lives, periods that seem to hold no promise. These periods cause us to dread the future. Fearing the future only brings more awful times.

Challenges are opportunities for advancement, for increased self-awareness and for self-fulfillment. We can face any situation knowing we have the strength. We need challenges in order to grow. With growth, self-esteem becomes stronger, along with belief in ourselves.

We often forget that we have an inner source of strength to meet every situation. A positive attitude is the result of deciding that we can make the right decisions, and having confidence in ourselves to do just that.

We have to determine where we want to go before we can decide how to get there. People have the tendency to let things happen to them, instead of making things happen. We passively go from one day to the next, letting external factors run our lives.

Looking at life this way may mean that we have to change the way we think and the way we live our lives. Many of us must get rid of already existing pain, since holding on to that pain makes it difficult to conquer our challenges.

Be a Survivor

Instead of reviewing specific theories on how to be a survivor, let's look at some survivors. The women profiled in this book have not only survived, they have found those castles in the sky we all search for and seldom find. They did not get there the easy way. No, there were no glass slippers for them. Barbra Streisand was raised by an emotionally absent mother and an abusive stepfather. Oprah Winfrey was initially abandoned by both her parents and, when finally reclaimed by her mother, was subjected to sexual abuse by family members. Drew Barrymore's father abandoned her at birth and, upon his return, was emotionally and physically abusive, sending Drew into a world of alcohol and drugs. Halle Berry, also abandoned by her father, grew up with low self-esteem, making her vulnerable to one abusive relationship after another. And Demi Moore moved from one place to another, only to lose the man whom she thought was her father, first through divorce and then from suicide.

These survivors have all been to hell and back; they have struggled to get to where they are today. However difficult their pasts may have been, these women are not victims. They may have been victimized in the past, but they have chosen to leave those lives behind and become survivors. Many people who are victimized remain victims all their lives. They decide that they don't have control over their lives, and that things just happen to them. They relinquish responsibility. After all, nothing in their lives is under their control, and therefore nothing is their fault. Situations they initiate are not their responsibility because environmental events drive their actions, not free will. This is a dangerous mindset to have. It gives others permission to use and abuse you, and it gives you permission to be irresponsible.

Those who are survivors have decided that, although what happened to them may not have been under their control, they now have control and will not be victimized again. They take responsibility for their lives and their accomplishments. If something goes wrong, it is up to them to fix it, and not to wallow in self-pity crying, "Why did his happen to me?" A survivor looks at the experience and evaluates what has happened in order to resolve any emotional issues caused by the experience and to avoid such future happenings. Survivors are not only capable of accomplishing the average, but they will excel—as women, as professionals, as human beings. These are survivors. Victims step aside.

Coping with Adversity

Coping through the hard times and handling the aftermath are important. These famous survivors found within themselves something special. Each knew that one day the hard times would end, giving her the opportunity to develop a life worth living. We all have something special within ourselves. Some believe this and are able to find it. Others don't. Some believe there is nothing worthwhile about themselves and therefore nothing valuable in their lives.But survivors know that things will change for the better and that they have what it takes to make that change.

When your environment is hostile and lacks nurturing and support, you have to find strength within yourself. What you look for or what you do could be something small. Something that seems simple can be built upon. These survivors all found talents, fantasies, beliefs, and the desire to live and be something better than the situations into which they had been born. All of them are smart—not necessarily formally educated, but smart. They have the kind of smarts you could never learn in a classroom. It is the kind of smarts that one learns from believing in oneself and experiencing life to its fullest. It is the kind of smarts that brings about wisdom. Each of us must find our own way of using that wisdom to cope with adverities in our own lives, motivating us on. We can look to these survivors as guides for motivation.

Motivation for Those Moments

Motivation is needed to go beyond bad experiences. Once you have coped with a situation, no matter how chronic and long-lived, you must be motivated to go beyond where you are. Successful survivors want more than what has been dictated by a situation or circumstance, more than just coping with difficulties. They know that there is something special in them, and they will use it to get what they want.

As the saying goes, "What doesn't kill you will make you strong." The harder the hardship, the stronger the survivor. This is not to minimize issues that linger from the past. They will be as big a burden as you let them be. They are painful, and you would like to ignore them and go on with your life. You can't. They are a part of you. Use them to motivate yourself. Don't let them weigh yourself down and hold you back with emotional baggage. Let that castle in the sky be your motivator, but don't sit around waiting for a prince to slip on a glass slipper and turn your world into a fairy tale. It's not going to happen. If you want that castle, you need to put on your boots and start hiking toward your dream.

Lessons Learned

Our experiences have taught us many lessons. These lessons are invaluable. If used to an advantage, they will make us wise. If we let them dictate and control our lives, we will revictimize ourselves. Lessons learned are gifts. They are the positives from negatives. We learn something from every moment in life. How you interpret each moment and choose to keep it in your memory will decide whether the past experience will help you or hinder you. The way you interpret the past will determine whether you learn something positive from an experience or whether you develop emotional issues that will haunt you, and that may eventually destroy you. How you interpret and integrate these experiences and the lessons they have to offer will decide what type of person you will become.

As humans, we are simply containers full of experiences. Take away our experiences, and we are nothing. Your personality is the accumulation of your experiences. Your personality type is the accumulation of how you use your experiences. Theses experiences and their lessons form your interpretation of yourself and the world. Experiences are the essence of your being.

Needless to say, Oprah, Barbara, Drew, Halle, and Demi are survivors. They have used lessons learned from the traumas and hardships of their lives as motivating forces, and not as hindrances. They have not only survived but have done well professionally and personally. Am I saying that all is well with them? No. But they have been and are continuing to strive toward perfection. They will have bumps along the way. This will be the case as long as they are alive. But they handle life's bumps well. If they are knocked off their feet, they get right back up, swinging. They do it so well that some may think their lives are trouble-free. This is not the case now, nor has it ever been. These women have had more then their share of troubles. Their hardships span the spectrum of traumas. Among them, they have experienced physical and sexual abuse, neglect, abandonment, drug and alcohol use, domestic violence, and poverty. No glass slippers here; their childhoods and their struggles to escape their environments were anything but fairy tales. Admire these women and, most importantly, learn from them.

2

Live!

"Dance like no one is watching.
Sing like no one is listening.
Love like you've never been hurt,
And live like it's heaven on Earth."
—Mark Twain

Before we look at the lives of the survivors described in this book, and the circumstances they survived, let's take a look at ourselves. There are elements in our lives we all have to deal with. Some are more common than others and occur more frequently as challenges or obstacles. The most common types of challenges are keeping our lives simple, making choices, controlling and understanding our emotions, and learning to trust and have healthy relationships.

Keep Life Simple

We often complicate our lives. We put forth obstacles that don't exist. We worry and wonder our way into a state of confusion. Then we get anxious over that state. We begin to obsess over these thoughts, and we become preoccupied with them. We try to figure out the what-ifs. We then continue to complicate situations until we realize we are overcomplicating things and should back off and keep things simple.

For every problem there is a solution. The solution is usually simpler than we realize. We have a tendency to go around the block to get across the street, especially if we think the street may be difficult to cross. Our greatest lesson in life is to keep it simple and to know that every problem has a solution.

We discover again and again that the solution to any problem may become apparent when we stop searching for it. The guidance we need for handling any difficulty, great or small, comes into focus when we remove the barriers. The greatest barrier is our frantic effort to solve the problem. We clutter our minds with complex possibilities. We don't stop long enough or become quiet enough to see the direction we must take to find the solution.

The Choices Are Yours

There are many choices in life. The day ahead offers us choices of many kinds, some big, some small. Many will affect persons close to us. A few will have profound effects on our destiny. But no choice and no decision we make will destroy our lives. Choices and decisions may be a result of us finding ourselves in bad relationships, worse jobs and financial difficulties. We look to maladaptive ways of dealing with our problems through drugs, alcohol and other behaviors which are self destructive. This makes things difficult, but not insurmountable. A particular decision may lead us slightly astray, or perhaps down a dead-end path, but we can always turn around and choose again.

We are offered opportunities again and again to make the right choices. The first step in making the right choice is to have the courage to choose and to be prepared to accept the consequences. You may need to take steps to correct the consequences, but at least you made a choice. The only wrong choice is not to choose.

Emotions: Can't Live without Them

We can expect to feel fear, even dread, at some points in our lives. Sometimes it feels as though it is more than we can bear. But the clouds will lift and things will clear. We are never given more than we can handle, and with each passing day, we can become more at ease with ourselves and with what life gives us. We can learn that bad times are temporary. Bad times only become permanent when you choose to let them be.

Remember that there is nothing unusual about being anxious, since everyone is anxious at one time or another. It is the way people handle their anxiety that makes the difference. It is how you interpret and decide whether to decrease or eliminate the anxiety that will make your anxiety less or more, or sometimes nonexistent. It helps to explore why you feel anxious and come to terms with it. If you tend to overreact when you are under stress and feel anxious, learn to identify what makes you overreact. Even if things are as bad as you think, your fearful thoughts weaken your ability to change things for the better. Put your anxiety to work for you. Anxiety directed toward a solution will sometimes make you more productive and aware of what you are doing. Or, if you choose, it can paralyze you. You cannot always manage external events, but you can manage your own thoughts and the way you react to those events. The choice, again, is up to you. You decide your path and action.

It is important for you to get in touch with your feelings, particularly your unconscious impulses. You may find that you are uneasy with your emotions and impulses. But this is what makes you human.

Be especially careful with your anger. This emotion tends to get out of control if you let it. Step back and analyze why you get angry, how it paralyzes you, and how it alienates people.

To be alive means to experience difficulties, conflicts, and challenges from many directions. How we react emotionally to adverse conditions determines and is determined by who we are. Resistance heightens the adversity. Accepting the condition and trusting all the while that we can handle it and learn from it, offers the opportunity to benefit from such an experience and ensures us that we will be all right.

Trust Is a Frightening Thing

Work on becoming more trusting. There are several people in your life you can turn to who care about you and who are trustworthy. If this is not the case, search for someone who can be trusted. Surely there is a person you know who is trustworthy.

Don't be afraid to get close to someone. This will mean risking rejection and stirring up some of your deepest fears, but the risk is worth taking. As humans, we have access to the gift of socialization, but because of past experiences, we are sometimes afraid of making a commitment. You may also fear that a commitment made to you may be broken, hurting you once again.

Look around and reflect on how your life has been influenced by persons close to you. Become aware that your presence affects their lives as well. Most of us could not have predicted the events and individuals that have influenced us. Nor can we anticipate what the future may hold. Trust that it will be all right.

At times we may feel that we have been victimized. Being victimized shocks both your body and your emotions. Even worse is the way being victimized can shatter our basic beliefs about ourselves, human nature, and the order of our world. The shattering of these beliefs greatly increase psychological distress. Any anxiety, confusion, or depression afterward is heightened by thoughts such as, "Who should I trust now?" and "What should I believe in?"

Victims are usually forced to reconsider these three areas about themselves and the world: vulnerability, world order, and personal strength. Before someone is victimized, that person often believes he or she is personally invulnerable, that the world is orderly and meaningful, and that he or she is a good, strong person. When someone is victimized, these beliefs are shattered, and there is a loss of invulnerability.

You may have thought at one time that something so awful could never happen to you. But then it did. Because of this, you no longer feel safe. At the very least, you feel less safe than you did before. And since it happened once, you fear it will happen again. The fear of vulnerability may develop into a list of symptoms, a sense of doom, or a foreshortened future.

There is the loss of an orderly world. Why did this happen? And why did it happen to me? You feel you didn't deserve it. You may conclude that life is meaningless and incomprehensible. Or you may conclude that you were singled out for pain and punishment because in some way you deserved what happened. You may feel that you are deficient, bad, or unworthy. None of this is true.

When someone is victimized, there is a loss of self-image. Being victimized usually brings to the forefront people's feelings of helplessness, vulnerability, and powerlessness. Consequently, they find themselves becoming more dependent on others at a time when they feel less trusting. This increases feelings of anxiety.

Vulnerability is as much a part of being human as is strength. Our vulnerability prevents us from becoming hard, brittle, and self-serving. Even when we are feeling vulnerable, we can choose to invite others into our lives and ask them to include us in theirs.

When you were young, you were encouraged to be strong. You were encouraged to be independent. Now, as adults, we often struggle to ask for help. Hopefully, as we grow and understand our human needs, we become more aware of what is available, and the difficulty of reaching out to others will be eased.

Life is full of dangers, risks, and challenges. We can choose to meet them with anxiety or with courage and confidence. To choose anxiety is to set yourself up for failure from the start. Doing so will prevent you from doing your best, for you will be using energy to focus on avoiding a feared situation rather than on tackling the task at hand. Life holds both dangers and rewards. How we react to both will determine how they affect our lives.

Relationships: The Fruit of Life

Remember that the world is not against you. Many people in your life care about you and look up to you. But when you are fixed on keeping them at bay or on controlling the interaction between you and them, you make it difficult for people to be close to you. Letting people in and allowing yourself to be vulnerable does not make you weak. It takes a strong person to take the risk. Believing that others are against you and reacting as such will only alienate you from those who could be your allies. Give credit to those who are on your side, and let them know how important they are to you.

It is good to be self-reliant, but there will be times when everyone must rely on someone. You may want to limit the number of people you depend on, making your life simpler, but total self-sufficiency is an illusion.

Wisdom from the Wise

Wisdom comes from the experiences we have and the lessons learned from those experiences. Just being alive and having experiences will not make you wise. If you go through life jumping from one experience to another without learning anything useful, you are wasting precious time.

Knowing that others have survived experiences equally devastating gives us hope, but it does not diminish our own personal suffering. Nor should it. Out of suffering comes new understanding. What we have experienced, both the good and the bad, is unique to ourselves. Even though each of us is unique, there are others who have experienced similar situations—similar enough for us to learn from their struggles. Our experiences can be shared. And by sharing, we lessen the power experiences have over us and others.

Through our experiences, we may become hardened, or we may become more empathetic. Even if we believe we are victims and that we have been wronged, true as that may be, we still need to decide to let it go. Holding on to it and all of the negative energy such a belief creates will only make us bitter and angry. Move past the experience and, if necessary, leave behind people who seem to encourage you to hold on to your bad experiences. Looking at an experience as a lesson learned, however painful that experience may have been, will add to your image of yourself as a survivor, as someone who is victorious. This approach will give you the courage and the optimism you need to continue your life with hope.

There is purpose in our lives. The ups and downs serve as growth. We must be sure not to get stuck in either state. If we do, it will interfere with our ability to move on. Learn from each experience because each experience has a valuable lesson to teach and is an opportunity to learn. Exert yourself. Force yourself to pay attention to what is going on with you and with your life.

Experience and the lessons learned through these experiences is wisdom. Wisdom is power. Having power through wealth, position, or simple brute force may allow people to do whatever they want, to feel important, to be feared and obeyed, but it will not give them peace. This type of power is superficial. When the lights go out at night, and it is only you with yourself, what counts is how comfortable you feel about your present company.

We have been blessed with unique qualities. There is no one like each one of us. We each have special personality traits that are projected in only the way each of us projects them. Each of us is perfect in our own uniqueness. We are all valuable and important in our own way. When we accept ourselves as special and different we find living with ourselves easier. How much more can be gained from life in the comfort of ourselves.

No Cinderella

There is no Cinderella. Replace your fantasies with wisdom. Hoping that some person or some miraculous event will rescue you and put you in a safe and secure place where all your needs will be fulfilled is a fantasy. No one or nothing will remove you from an uncomfortable situation. Only you can relieve yourself from your pain. You are the miracle. Your castle exists within yourself. If we listen to ourselves, to our innermost voices, we know that we have the power to heal ourselves. Self-healing begins with making our own decisions about what we are and what we want to do and deciding that we will be true to ourselves.

When you look at the lives of famous people, these people seem to have it all, and their lives seem to imply that Cinderella does exist. For each of these people, we think, some miraculous event occurred and the glass slipper found its way to his or her feet. You may know that some of these famous people came from humble beginnings, but surely they never experienced anything as horrific and painful as you have. Their beginnings could not have contained the hardships that you have endured. If so, they would not be where they are today. Not so. Some famous celebrities have been fortunate, but for most it has been hard work. There is no glass slipper. There are only hiking boots.

Change and wisdom brings about miracles. When we are troubled by circumstances in our lives, a change is called for. We must initiate change. When we reflect on our past, we remember that the changes we most dreaded again and again have positively influenced our lives in untold ways. Everything changes; nothing stays the same. Letting go of the way things are, anticipating instead what they might become, frees us to live each moment fully. What life has given us may not be what we dreamed it would be. Life's lessons may not be those we would have chosen to learn.

Wisdom dictates how we will spend our lives. Wisdom comes with time and only with time because only the experiences that come with time foster wisdom. It is up to you to decide whether it will be wisdom that you gain throughout your life, or fear.

Acceptance of our past and the conditions in our lives that we could not change brings relief. It gives us the peace we so often seek. We cannot change the past, but we can learn from it and then put the past behind us. Each day is a new beginning and offers us a chance to look ahead with hope.

3

The Hansel and Gretel Experience

Fairytales are more than entertainment. They relay valuable information and lessons in the form of fables. We usually read fairytales to children to amuse them. Sometimes we read fairtales to children to frighten them as a form of entertainment. Seldom do we read them with the intention of gaining insight into ourselves and our world. Maybe we should.

In a great forest, there was a poor woodcutter with his wife and his two children. The boy was called Hansel and the girl Gretel, who we will rename Barbra and brother. They were the stepchildren of the woodcutter's wife. The woodcutter was poor and had a hard time feeding his family. He thought this over by night in his bed, tossing and turning about in his anxiety. He groaned and said to his wife, "What is to become of us? How are we to feed our poor children when we no longer have anything even for ourselves?"

"I'll tell you what, husband," answered the woman, "early tomorrow morning we will take the children out into the forest to where it is the thickest. There we will light a fire for them and give each of them one more piece of bread, and then we will go to our work and leave them alone. They will not find the way home again, and we shall be rid of them."

"No, wife," said the man, "I will not do that. How can I bear to leave my children alone in the forest?"

"Oh, you fool!" said she. "Then we must all die of hunger," and she left him no peace until he consented.

The two children had not been able to sleep because of their hunger pains and had heard what their stepmother had said to their father. Brother wept bitter tears and said to Barbra, "Now all is over with us."

"Do not distress yourself. I will soon find a way to help us," Barbra said. And when the old folks had fallen asleep, she got up, put on her little coat, opened the door below, and crept outside. The moon shone brightly, and the white pebbles that lay in front of the house glittered like real silver pennies. Barbra stooped and stuffed the little pocket of her coat with as many as she could get in. When day dawned, but before the sun had risen, the woman came and awoke the two children, saying, "Get up. We are going into the forest to fetch wood." She gave each a little piece of bread, and said, "There is something for your dinner, but do not eat it up before then, for you will get nothing else."

Brother took the bread under his jacket because Barbra had the pebbles in her pocket. Then they all set out together on the way to the forest. When they had walked a short time, Barbra stood still and peeped back at the house, and did so again and again. Each time, Barbra threw one of the white pebbles from her pocket onto the road.

When they had reached the middle of the forest, the father said, "Now, children, pile up some wood, and I will light a fire so you will not be cold." Barbra and Brother gathered brushwood together, as high as a little hill. The brushwood was lighted, and when the flames were burning very high, the woman said, "Now, children, lie down by the fire and rest. We will go into the forest and cut some wood. When we are done, we will come back and fetch you away."

Barbra and Brother sat by the fire, and when noon came, each ate a little piece of bread. And since they had been sitting such a long time, their eyes closed with fatigue, and they fell fast asleep. When they awoke, it was already night. Brother began to cry and said, "How are we to get out of the forest now?" But Barbra comforted him and said, "Just wait a little, until the moon has risen, and then we will soon find the way." And when the full moon had risen, Barbra took her little brother by the hand and followed the pebbles, which shone like newly coined silver pieces, showing them the way.

They walked the whole night long, and by break of day, came once more to their father's house. They knocked at the door, and when the woman opened it and saw that it was Barbra and Brother, she said, "You naughty children, why have you slept so long in the forest? We thought you were never coming back at all!" The father, however, rejoiced, for it had cut him to the heart to leave them behind alone.

Again the parents planned to take the children into the woods and leave them. Early in the morning, the woman came and took the children out of their beds. She gave each of them a piece of bread, but the pieces were smaller than the time before. On the way into the forest, Barbra crumbled the bread in her pocket and threw a morsel on the ground. Little by little, Barbra threw all the crumbs on the path.

The woman led the children still deeper into the forest, where they had never in their lives been before, and left them there. When the moon came, the two children set out, but they found no crumbs, for the many thousands of birds that fly about in the woods and fields had picked them all up.

Barbra said to Brother, "We shall soon find the way," but they did not find it. They walked the whole night and all the next day, too, from morning till evening, but they did not get out of the forest. They were very hungry, for they had nothing to eat but two or three berries, which grew near the ground. And as they were so weary that their legs would carry them no longer, they lay down beneath a tree and fell asleep.

It was now three mornings since they had left their father's house. They began to walk again, but they always came deeper into the forest, and if help did not come soon, they would die of hunger and weariness. Finally, they reached a little house. When they approached the little house, they saw that it was built of bread and covered with cakes. "We will set to work on that," said Barbra, "and have a good meal." Barbra reached up and broke off a little of the roof to see how it tasted, and Brother leaned against the window and nibbled at the panes.

Suddenly the door opened, and a woman as old as the hills came creeping out. Barbra and Brother were so terribly frightened that they dropped what they were eating. The old woman, however, nodded her head, and said, "Oh, you dear children, who has brought you here? Do come in, and stay with me. No harm shall happen to you."

The old woman had only pretended to be kind. She was in reality a wicked witch, who lay in wait for children, and had only built the little house of bread in order to entice them there. When children fell into her power, she killed them, then cooked and ate them. She seized Brother with her shriveled hand, carried him into a little stable, and locked him in behind a grated door. Scream as he might, it would not help him. Then she went to Barbra, shook her till she woke, and cried, "Get up, lazy thing. Fetch some water and cook something good for your brother. He is in the stable outside and is to be made fat. When he is fat, I will eat him." Barbra began to weep bitterly, but it was all in vain, for she was forced to do what the wicked witch commanded.

While Barbra was preparing the oven to cook her brother as the witch had ordered, the witch pushed poor Barbra out to the oven, from which flames of fire were already darting. "Creep in," said the witch, "and see if it is properly heated, so that we can put the bread in." And once Barbra was inside, the witch intended to shut the oven and let her bake in it, and then she would eat her, too. But Barbra saw what she had in mind, and said, "I do not know how I am to do it; how do I get in?" The witch said, "The door is big enough; just look, I can get in myself!" and she crept close to the oven. Then Barbra gave her a push that drove her far into it, shut the iron door, and fastened the bolt. Oh, then the witch began to howl quite horribly, but Barbra ran away, and the witch burned to death.

Barbra ran like lightning to Brother, opened his little stable, and cried, "Brother, we are saved! The old witch is dead."

They began to walk. The forest became more and more familiar to them, and, at length, they saw their father's house and began to run. They rushed into the parlor and threw themselves around their father's neck. The man had not known one happy hour since he had left the children in the forest. The woman had died, so the father and the children lived together in perfect happiness.

Truth or fantasy? It's unthinkable, but it has happened, a parent sacrificing their children to save a romantic relationship. This is unbelievable for most, but it happens more often than we would like to think. There are many abusive relationships where children are sacrificed for the "good" of the parents' relationship.

Although children may be vulnerable, they are also resilient. The abused and neglected often have an inner strength they tap into, a strength that allows them to tolerate or escape (at least mentally) the abusive environment. Children may dissociate into a world in which they feel safe and secure.

The ability to forgive is strong in children. They often forgive the injustices done to them by their parents. Abused children often choose to return to or stay with their parents, even though they have been abused. They then make excuses for their parents' behavior or blame themselves.

Some children become strong. In surviving the abuse or neglect, they become fighters, warding off those who would victimize them. Choosing not to relive the abuse, these children find a way to escape it and make their lives better.

Children should not have to choose between becoming a victim or a survivor. Children need protection and security. The world is full of danger. There are predators waiting to harm them. But there are also others who will help. Children's care and safety should be guaranteed. But this is not always the case, and so we deal with the consequences.

4

Barbra Streisand: A Queen in Her Glory

"You have got to discover you, what you do, and trust it."
—Barbra Streisand

When We Were a Family

Barbra Streisand was born in Brooklyn, New York, on April 24, 1942. Her parents, Emanuel and Diana Streisand, had Barbra twelve years after they were married. It appeared that Diana had the life she had always wanted, with a husband and children she loved.

Emanuel "Manny" Streisand was a man who outwardly appeared to be healthy. He had a lot of energy and liked athletic activities. After the arrival of his daughter, Barbra, in 1942, he decided to take a summer job as a counselor at Camp Cascade in Highmount, New York. This meant moving the family to Highmount and spending the entire season in the Catskill Mountains, far from Brooklyn.

The counselor position was strenuous for Manny. He had previous medical problems dating back to when he and Diana married, and they now began to cause trouble. Manny had been in a car accident that left him with chronic headaches. He had epileptic seizures, which could happen at any time. After Manny began his camp job, his headaches became much worse. One day, the headache was so bad he passed out. He was left alone to rest. When he failed to awaken, he was taken to the hospital. Within twenty-four hours of being admitted to the hospital, Manny was dead—on August 4, 1943. The cause of death was kept a secret from his children. They were told that he died from a cerebral hemorrhage, the result of overwork. He actually died from an epileptic seizure following a head injury he had received while working at the camp.

Diana was so traumatized by the death of her husband that she was unable to express anything but grief; she became emotionally unavailable. Manny's untimely death left Barbra with no parental support: her father had died, and her mother was unable to live. Barbra had lost both her parents.

Unable to support her children, Diana moved back to Brooklyn to live with her parents. They lived in a small, unattractive, three-room apartment located in a poor area of Brooklyn. Diana's parents slept in one room, Diana and Barbra shared a bed in another room, and Barbra's brother slept on a folding cot in the third room. They did not have a living room where the family could gather and be with one another socially. The home's function was as a roof over their heads. Barbra's mother continued to wallow in her grief and withdraw from her children.

Diana's family was rigid, dispassionate, and more likely to dispense punishment than affection or approval. Everybody had a role to fill, and there was little room for mistakes. The boundaries were clearly drawn. One of the first words Barbra learned was no. When she did make mistakes, Barbra would hide under a table to avoid severe scoldings and beatings that could follow.

Because of her mother's depression, Barbra had a lot to deal with. Diana's depression affected the way she interacted with her children. Children of depressed and withdrawn mothers tend to blame themselves for their mothers' reactions to them. They began to feel guilty about situations they did not cause. This guilt is associated with children's need to help a parent who rejects their help. As children get older, they start to suppress the guilt. The guilt turns into unrealistic fears and interferes with the children's ability to be empathic with others, increasing their interpersonal distance and their vulnerability to depression.

A parent who is unemotionally unavailable or distant exhibits behaviors that produce a maladaptive environment. When Barbra and other children of emotionally unbalanced parents become adults, they use what they have learned as a guide. They too often exhibit behaviors that are reactions to the environment in which they were raised. Their perception is skewed, and they find it difficult to review their behavior in order to decide whether they need to correct it.

In the process of developing from childhood to adulthood, people decide which of the values they have learned will remain important and which ones they will modify based on their experience. People may also use what they have experienced in a way that causes them to become rigid and inflexible, making it hard to modify and integrate socially at the adult level.

Barbra's mother was emotionally neglectful toward Barbra and her brother. Emotional neglect or failure to provide an environment in which children can thrive, learn, and develop, is one of the most difficult forms of abuse to identify because of its subtle manifestations. Some forms of emotional neglect include ignoring a child, rejecting a child, pushing the child away, and isolating the child. When any of these happen, the child may develop a poor self-image, become overly shy and/or needy, be afraid to go home, or become overly passive-aggressive, and/or demanding.

Barbra loved to be away from her home. She would leave every chance she got. She found school and a friend's home to be her refuges, allowing her to escape from what she considered a hostile environment fueled by neglect.

Barbra's pain could not be seen on the outside. The emotional neglect she experienced from her mother was the most difficult part of her existence. A child can easily be hurt by what is lacking. Emotional neglect hurts as much as physical abuse, but it doesn't leave marks on the outsides of children. And because neglect leaves no observable damage, people tend to ignore it, and the emotional abuse or neglect continues.

Emotional neglect happens when children don't receive the love and attention they need to feel good about themselves. Children need to hear praise and supportive statements, including how much they are loved. If their parents lack affection to the point where they cannot give their children this kind of support, it is detrimental for the child. Children may appear to be cared for on the outside but may not be receiving the love and attention they need to support their emotional needs.

Barbra was fearful that when her mother went to work she was not going to return home at night. Barbra had learned that parents sometimes don't return. Her father didn't. When her mother did return home, she was always tired and too impatient to tolerate her children. She would dismiss them not because of a lack of love but because of a lack of energy.

Barbra found all sorts of ways to entertain herself. She played tea party and dress-up, spending hours experimenting with her mother's makeup. She also loved to sing. She would spend a good part of her day singing in the halls of her apartment building. She dissociated herself from her environment. It was the only way she could protect and shield herself.

Barbra didn't have any toys to play with. All she had was a hot water bottle with a little sweater on it that she used as a doll. Barbra would retreat into her own fantasy world where little girls had tea sets and party dresses, and where parents gave them attention. Her fantasy world was different from her home life. It was a difficult situation for a young child, but Barbra made the best of it. What she couldn't get at home she made up in her head.

Barbra was glad to start school. It was an escape from the apartment she hated. Barbra enjoyed school because she could ask questions and receive attention. She had a friend whose home she would visit. They had a small television. Watching television introduced Barbra to the world outside of Brooklyn, a world she wanted to be a part of. Learning about this world opened her eyes to a world of laughter and excitement, a world that was the complete opposite of her own. It provided one of her earliest inspirations to become an actress. She used this inspiration to create a new perception of herself.

We each have ways in which we like to perceive ourselves. In many cases, self-image is carefully constructed and guarded. But sometimes there is a conflict between who we are and who we would like to be. Barbra saw no conflict; instead, she saw a goal.

For many, television is a means of identifying oneself and one's goals. It introduces possibilities that lie outside one's environment. People often seek television when they feel inadequate. Why? Because they can escape into it, becoming the characters they see and living the life they see on the screen. People are more likely to watch television when they are feeling bad about themselves than when they feel good about themselves.

Mom Needs a Husband

Barbra was diagnosed with anemia at age five. Her mother thought that a summer health camp would help, so during the summer of 1949, Barbra was sent off to Hebrew Health Camp. She hated it. She spent most of her time crying in an effort to go home.

Barbra's mother was busy while Barbra was at camp. She began dating and looking for a husband. Barbra hated all the suitors her mother dated and would throw a fit when any of them came to pick up her mother. This did not deter her mother.

Enter Louis Kind. Barbra knew that her mother was serious about him. Barbra was sure of this when she went to camp for the second time, and he accompanied them. Barbra protested angrily when they were ready to leave her at the camp. She did not want her mother to leave without her. Her mother gave in and the three of them drove back in complete silence.

Louis did not intend to marry Barbra's mother. Even when Diana announced that she was pregnant by him, he still did not want to marry her. He was still married and had to get a divorce from his first wife, and he did not want to immediately jump into another marriage.

When Diana's father, Barbra's grandfather, heard about the pregnancy, he insisted Diana and her two children leave his home. He was too rigid and unforgiving to tolerate his unmarried daughter's pregnancy. Diana moved into a one-bedroom apartment in Brooklyn. The apartment was cold, ugly, and cheap.

When Diana was nine months pregnant, Louis changed his mind and agreed to marry her. She gave birth to a baby girl, Rosalind. Things had to change now. Barbra was used to sleeping with her mother. She could no longer do this. It was bad enough that she had received little attention from her mother before Louis Kind, but now it was worse. Barbra already noticed more distancing between her mother and her.

Barbra woke up the first morning in their new apartment complaining that there was a clicking in her ears. When she told her mother about it, Barbra's mother and stepfather interpreted her complaint as manipulation for more attention. From that day on, Barbra did not mention the clicking in her ears. She developed tinnitus (a ringing in the ears) and wore scarves around her head to try to block out the sound. Barbra interpreted this condition as some kind of psychic warning. Two years later, the click turned into a high-pitched wail that has remained with her.

Louis doted on Rosalind but ignored and mistreated the rest of the family. He refused to support his family financially, claiming he had no money. He fought bitterly with Diana whenever he returned from his business trips and verbally abused both Barbra and Sheldon (Barbra's brother). Louis did not care who was around when he did this. He would demean and embarrass them in public. The verbal and emotional abuse turned to physical abuse.

The marriage between Mr. and Mrs. Kind was shrouded in fear. Barbra witnessed the hostility and violence inflicted on her mother by her stepfather. He wore down Diana's spirit and abused her body. Barbra vowed that she would never let a man do this to her. No man would ever make her feel insignificant and worthless.

Sometimes it was Barbra who suffered Louis's wrath. He would threaten and verbally abuse her. There was a lot of shouting and fighting in the house. Her stepfather would taunt her and tell her she wasn't pretty and would never amount to anything. Barbra would run away crying.

Louis's emotional abuse toward Barbra was severe. Emotional child abuse is maltreatment that may result in emotional problems later in life. It involves words, actions, and neglect, which may haunt the victim throughout his or her life if not resolved. Abusers constantly reject, ignore, belittle, dominate, and criticize their victims. This form of abuse may occur without physical abuse, but usually the physical abuse follows.

Louis frequently exposed Barbra to family violence and was unwilling or unable to provide affection or stimulation, except to his natural daughter. Barbra was exposed to many types of abuse, which included making excessive demands on her penalizing her for positive, normal behavior such as smiling, exploration, and vocalization. There was no parent/child bond between Louis and Barbra.

Being exposed to this type of interaction in the home may cause poor relationships with peers, lack of self-confidence, and unusual fears for the child. The child often finds it difficult to react emotionally or develop an emotional bond with others because of the fear of what will happen in the relationship.

Barbra did not have the opportunity to look at her home as a safe and secure place to run to for comfort. The walls of her apartment were her prison, and she spent most of her young life with her hands clasped behind her head, staring at the ceiling, plotting and dreaming of the day she would escape.

As children, we learn to survive. We repress and distort the bad in our lives to protect ourselves from what may hurt us. Reactions to hostile environments live on in children as they become adults. We live life reacting to childhood wounds, continuing to try to get the healthy attention, affection, love, and nurturing we should have had as children.

With all that we have to handle as adults, it is important to take notice that the most destructive type of abuse is the emotional abuse we learn to inflict upon ourselves. We judge and shame ourselves, continuing the abuse. We incorporate the messages we learned from the behavior of others into our relationship with ourselves. We emotionally abuse ourselves on a daily basis because we don't have healthy self-esteem. If we had healthy self-esteem, we would not allow anyone to emotionally abuse us, including ourselves.

Emotional abuse is devastating. Bruises to the body fade away. Bruises to the heart and soul stay. Emotional abuse is damaging to one's self-esteem and sets a person up to become trapped in the vicious, self-perpetuating cycles of shame, suffering, and self-abuse that drive the dynamics of psychological problems later in life.

Emotional abuse systematically wears away at the victim's self-confidence, sense of self-worth, trust in perceptions, and self-concept. Emotional abuse may occur through constant berating and belittling, intimidation, or adopting a mask of love and pretending to provide care-giving gestures. Regardless of the method, the results are harmful. Eventually, the recipient of the abuse loses all sense of personal worth. The abuse eats away at the victim's self-esteem.

Sometimes victims blame themselves for the abuse. Thinking that they are worthless and the source of everything bad, they take on responsibility for the perpetrator, the abuser. This self-blame can extend to relationships with peers. Barbra was picked on frequently by other children because she looked different. She did not like this rejection, which was evident to others, motivating them to pick on her even more. Like many abused children, Barbra thought that, in some way, it was her fault. After all, she had heard this time and time again in her own home. Her stepfather once told her that she could not have an ice cream cone because she was ugly. He taunted her continually, telling her how plain she was compared to her sister. And now the children in her school were following suit.

Louis possessed characteristics common to an abusing adult. He blamed and belittled Barbra, described her negatively, made her feel as if she were at fault, had unrealistic expectations of her, openly admitted to disliking or hating her, threatened her with severe punishment, withdrew comfort as a means of discipline, and was emotionally cold and unsupportive. In addition, he possessed a violent nature.

The consequences of emotional abuse linger. Abuse can be serious and long-term. As teenagers, abused individuals often find it difficult to trust, participate in, and achieve happiness in interpersonal relationships. They may have difficulty resolving complex feelings left over from their childhood. Louis had left his mark on the entire Streisand family.

Barbra observed the lack of love between her mother and her stepfather. Her mother and stepfather did not share love in a healthy way, if they shared it at all. The hostile love in their relationship was the kind of love Barbra witnessed and learned from.

When children grow up in a household like this, where love is displayed in an unhealthy way, they view love as critical, shaming, manipulative, controlling, and abusive. But relief was at hand. Louis Kind was absent frequently from the family and left them for good in 1956. This was a dream come true for Barbra.

Barbra handled the abuse issues by turning them into physical symptoms. She retreated into her own world and began to complain about being ill. Her hypochondria intensified as she started to convince herself that she had cancer and a heart condition. One day, she saw a pamphlet on cancer that listed the symptoms. She convinced herself she had every one of them. She had convinced herself that she only had six months to live. Within days, she developed psychosomatic symptoms.

Now that Louis kind was gone, Barbra could now concentrate on herself. Barbra was not who she wanted to be, which was defined by her "ideal self." An ideal self is a set of personal goals and expectations we have for ourselves. Barbra's self-image was based on what she was told about herself during her interactions with her mother, stepfather, and grandparents. Her ideal self was based on television images of stars. The difference between her ideal image and her self-image produced a disturbing gap.

Barbra was comparing her self-image with the external images of movie stars and entertainers she saw on television and at the movies. Her view of herself was shaped by her unique thoughts and beliefs. She saw herself in both positive and negative ways according to these beliefs, and both were biased.

To overcome the negative feelings produced by a gap such as this, one must reduce the gap between self-expectations (ideal self) and self-perceptions (self-image). We can either change ourselves to become more like our self-expectations, or we can change our self-expectations to better match what we have become.

In order to move toward the ideal self, we must love ourselves unconditionally. Loving ourselves unconditionally means accepting all of the realities about ourselves and still loving ourselves. It is not that we must think we are perfect, but that we need to like what we see. How we see ourselves is sometimes warped by society's image of how one should be. Barbra was not the idealized image of a star, but look how far she has gone with that image. If you love yourself with confidence, others will follow you. Most people do not love and accept themselves. Love what you have, believe in it, and work with it.

Developing positive views of ourselves means that we believe in our own strengths, especially in our ability to motivate ourselves and do what will make us happy. This view of ourselves will help us go into almost any situation with a positive attitude and willingness to do whatever it takes to achieve happiness. Positive beliefs about ourselves can provide the energy, flexibility, and the stamina we need to handle what is thrown our way.

Having a positive self-image does not mean being perfect. When someone believes he or she must be the best to be okay, that belief inherently creates a vulnerable ego, constantly under attack and scrutiny. The goal is to be *your* best. When someone defines herself or himself by external conditions, this increases the person's vulnerability and produces conditions that are unhealthy. Only if we love ourselves unconditionally and define our own unique needs and goals will we be happy with ourselves.

Barbra had difficulties with her self-image because she spent hours in front of the television, mimicking actors and actresses, dreaming of the glamorous lives of the stars. She experimented with her mother's makeup and cigarettes, trying to manipulate her physical appearance into something that was acceptable to Barbra.

She clung to what she knew was acceptable: her voice. So Barbra sang and sang. Singing helped her escape not only the ringing in her ears but also a life she didn't want. Singing made her a star in her own mind, so she would sing every chance she got, anywhere she could. By the time she was ten, she was set on becoming a performer. Her entertainment aspirations were known to the few friends she made in her school.

In 1952, at age of ten, Barbra began to sing publicly. Her official debut was at a PTA meeting. She frequently heard people say, "That funny looking girl sure has a good voice." Her mother did not think Barbra was pretty enough to go into show business and discouraged her from pursuing a career in entertainment. Barbra didn't listen. She took ballet lessons, sang and danced in a hotel talent show, and auditioned for the Metro Goldwyn Mayer (MGM) motion picture studio. MGM offered Barbra a place in their training classes, but her mother refused to let her participate because Barbra would not be paid. Barbra was allowed to enter a talent contest while the family was on summer vacation at a hotel in the Catskill

Mountains. Barbra won the contest. She impressed a lot of people and received offers of work and later sang at weddings.

The acceptance she received from her singing helped her deal with the rejection she received in other areas of her life. By the time she entered high school at the age of thirteen, she was use to rejection. Her way of dealing with the rejection was to reject society before it could reject her. This was her way of controlling her environment and surviving in it. How did she accomplish this? She withdrew and lived her life for the future.

She had to preserve what little self-esteem she had left. Self-esteem, the opinion you have of yourself, is based on your attitude toward your value as a person, your achievement, and how you think others see you. It affects the perception you have about your purpose in life, your place in the world, your potential for success, and your social status. It affects how you relate to others. It is a measure of your independence or ability to stand on your own feet.

Developing a high degree of self-esteem is important to a person's well-being. If you have a high level of self-esteem, you will be confident and sure of yourself. You will be highly motivated and feel that you have the right to succeed. Without feeling this right, you may be stuck in constant conflict with yourself.

A young person's self-esteem will be higher if he or she is treated with respect. A child who is belittled, patronized, or put down will suffer from lack of confidence. But if given respect, a child will have more opportunity to develop a sense of trust and confidence. Barbra was constantly put down and labeled a failure. She received no respect in her home. She somehow found it within herself.

Barbra went to Erasmus High School in Brooklyn, which was known for its superior academic standards. When Barbra was in elementary school, she was in the Intellectually Gifted Opportunity Program. Because of this, she was put directly into honors classes in high school. She excelled academically. Socially she didn't fit in. Her classmates found her to be a loner, aloof, and self-centered.

While in high school, Barbra worked part-time at a Chinese restaurant. She wore silk kimonos and grew her nails long, polishing them bright red. Her noticeably long nails have remained one of her trademarks. Mrs. Choy, the owner of the restaurant, was close to Barbra and answered questions Barbra's mother did not seem interested in answering. They talked about love, life, and sex, and had discussions Barbra could never have had with her own mother.

Barbra wanted to be glamorous. She tried different hairstyles and various styles of clothing. Barbra's need for glamour cost money, so she took to shoplifting in an attempt to have enough money to be fashionable. She would walk around the store looking for discarded receipts, then gather the items on the receipts and take then back for a refund. She then would go to another store and buy what she wanted.

Barbra continued her singing. She took freshman chorus and was chosen to be a member of the choral club. The choral club accepted only the most talented students. Barbra auditioned twice for the choral club within several months and was rejected both times. But she was persistent. Barbra had an idea to record a tape to present to the director of the choir. She asked a pianist at the Catskills Hotel to record a professional tape of her singing. When the tape was complete, she auditioned again and was finally accepted into the choral club. She quit after two years. She felt that her talent was not being recognized.

Barbra continued to pursue her entertainment career. She went to Manhattan for her fourteenth birthday to see a production of *The Diary of Anne Frank*. Barbra was moved by the performance. She decided she wanted to perform like that. Now determined to be an actress, Barbra immediately began auditioning. She auditioned for the leading role in the play *Saint Joan*. Her readings went very well, but they wanted someone prettier. Barbra was devastated. This incident confirmed her mother's idea that Barbra could never make it as an entertainer because she was not good looking enough.

In an attempt to spare her daughter more pain, Barbra's mother began to actively dissuade her daughter from pursuing an acting career by emphasizing to Barbra that she did not have the looks for show business . Barbara continued to be rejected by directors because she wasn't pretty enough, which only strengthened her insecurities about her appearance.

This was a time when Barbra's home life was changing. In 1956, when Barbara was fourteen, her mother and Louis divorced. Barbra's mother and her family struggled to survive. After the divorce, her mother began working and Barbra spent her time persuing her goal of being glamorous.

Barbara's life soon changed for the better. Barbra landed a volunteer job as a backstage apprentice, sweeping floors at the Cherry Lane Theatre in Greenwich Village. Barbra was offered a scholarship to an acting class. A whole new world opened up for Barbra. She was accepted into a year-round apprenticeship program at the Cherry Lane Theatre. Her mother allowed her to participate on the condition that Barbra kept her grades up at school. Barbra complied.

During her internship, she met Allan Miller, a Manhattan acting coach. He was not impressed with her audition but saw talent. He was impressed by her enthusiasm, inquisitiveness, and forceful personality. She and Allan Miller became close friends.

In the summer of 1957, Barbra attended the Malden Playhouse in the Adirondacks in upstate New York. At the Malden Playhouse, she found the support she had sought. She was cast as Mille Owens, in *Kansas Picnic*, and as Elsa, a sexy secretary on the prowl, in *Desk Set*.

Choosing to Be Different

At seventeen, Barbra got her first acting job in Manhattan. She was cast as a tough, thirty-five-year-old woman, playing opposite a young Joan Rivers. The play, *Driftwood*, did not get a single review and closed after only six weeks. During the production of *Driftwood*, Barbra graduated from high school. She had no interest in going to college—she wanted to pursue acting.

Now Barbra was out of school and an adult. She knew that she was not stuck in the existence into which she had been born, and she had grown up. She knew that she did not have to be that "ugly girl." She had a strong powerful voice and was attractive enough to be cast in three plays. She had proven to herself and others that she was talented and that talent would take her far.

We have to watch those negative labels others give us or that we give ourselves. Negative self-labels can become self-fulfilling prophesies. Even positive labels can have negative effects if they are self-limiting. If we view ourselves as stuck in a certain situation and in a specific role, we will be threatened by change. If we view ourselves as growing, changing beings, then we will welcome change as a natural part of living our lives.

Barbra accepted change and knew the role she wanted to play in life. She held steadfast to the identity she was building for herself, an identity that was not influenced by what her parents or peers thought of her but was based on what she thought of herself.

Barbra's singing career was really taking off. After graduation, she packed her bags and moved to Manhattan where she could pursue acting full-time. She took all the obstacles her mother saw, her unconventional looks, her odd personality, and her self-defined way of dressing, and turned them into advantages.

While Barbra was intent on acting, it was her amazing vocal gift that first thrust her into the New York performance scene. At the age of eighteen, she was stunning audiences at clubs in Manhattan. She appeared regularly on late-night television talk/variety shows. She was a great hit with New York's gay community and also appeared in gay clubs.

In 1962, she signed a contract with Columbia Records. Her debut album quickly became the nation's top-selling record by a female vocalist. The album,

The Barbra Streisand Album, won two Grammy awards, including album of the year. At that time, she was the youngest artist to have won that title.

Barbra's first Broadway play, *I Can Get It for You Wholesale*, opened at the Winter Garden Theater on March 26, 1964. The play won her the New York Drama Critics Award, and she received a Tony nomination. It was after this musical that Barbra was signed for the part of comedienne Fanny Brice in the Broadway production of *Funny Girl*. The role won her a second Tony nomination. Her life had been changed forever.

She signed a ten-year contract with CBS Television to produce and star in television specials. The contract gave her complete artistic control, an unheard of concession to an artist so young and inexperienced. The first special, *My Name Is Barbra*, earned five Emmy awards, and the following four shows, including the memorable *Color Me Barbra*, earned critical praise and high audience ratings. It was re-released twenty years later and became an instant best seller in the video-cassette market.

Few movie debuts have been as successful as Barbra Streisand's in Columbia Pictures' *Funny Girl*. In addition to winning the 1968 Academy Award, she won a Golden Globe award and was named star of the year by the National Association of Theatre Owners.

Who would have thought, when she stood in front of the bathroom mirror in Brooklyn as a teen, that she would become such a hit. She was not a pretty girl, as her own mother reminded her often enough. Confidence was her friend and her motivator.

Her dreams did not come out of her body image but rather from her inner strength. Body image affects how you feel about yourself. It's an important factor in self-esteem for women, men, adolescents, and children. Self-esteem in women in particular seems to be dependent on how they think they look.

You have to realize that your image is unique. Focus on your good points. Once you start comparing yourself to others, you are doomed. There will always be someone who looks better.

Adolescents, teens, and young adults often fall into this trap by worrying about how they look, and by comparing themselves to their friends and others. Teenagers want to look like the stars and pop idols they see on television. So did Barbra. These stars are not average-looking people. Somewhere along the way, Barbra realized that it was okay just to be herself.

Oh! The Lights on Broadway

Barbra found a sense of self-worth. Having a sense of self-worth and confidence increases your ability to accomplish your goals. You need to believe that you deserve to live life as you want. This is not selfishness.

Lack of confidence feeds feelings of failure and inadequacy. You must think positive things about yourself and about what you have accomplished. Barbra fantasized about what she wanted in life and where she wanted to be. She then made her plans, moved forward, and never looked back.

Barbra overcame the obstacles that she had no control over by focusing on her strengths and using them. You will succeed if you are true to yourself. Most people have no problem listing their weaknesses, but when asked what their strengths are, they have difficulty identifying them. Be true to yourself in recognizing both your strengths and your weaknesses. Barbra identified her goals and worked at achieving them. If you do the same, your confidence will increase and you will feel positive about yourself and your life. Barbra did her best at everything she tried. She went after her goals with focus and determination. She didn't think about why she couldn't accomplish her goals; she only thought about how to do it.

Barbra was creative with her achievements and accomplished a lot of firsts. She starred in and directed *The Prince of Tides*, which was the first motion picture directed by its star to receive a nomination for best director from the Directors Guild of America. The movie also received seven Academy Award nominations. In addition to the recognition and awards she received for her first Broadway appearance in *I Can Get It for You Wholesale* and for her first record album, *The Barbra Streisand Album*, she won the 1968 Academy Award for best actress, the first of two Oscars for her motion picture debut in *Funny Girl*. She became the first woman ever to produce, direct, write, and star in a major motion picture with *Yentl*. *Yentl* took fourteen years of development before it became a reality. Now that's focus and determination.

Barbra was honored with an Emmy Award and the distinguished Peabody Award for her first television special, *My Name Is Barbra*. The program earned a total of five Emmys. She repeated this achievement thirty years later with a musical production for television, *Barbra Streisand: The Concert*, and received two additional Emmy awards among the five for the production.

After appearing in the films *Hello, Dolly!* and *On a Clear Day You Can See Forever*, she starred in the comedy *The Owl and the Pussycat*. The year 1972 brought another comedy hit, *What's Up Doc?* followed by *Up the Sandbox*. The latter was one of the first American films to deal with the growing women's movement. It was the premiere picture for her production company, Barwood Films.

The Way We Were earned her a 1973 Academy Award nomination for best actress. *A Star Is Born*, released in 1976, with her as a producer, won six Golden Globes. The soundtrack album was certified as multiplatinum.

A ten-year contract with CBS Television to produce and star in television specials punctuated her acceptance as a formable force. Throughout the next four decades, Streisand achieved superstardom both as an actress and as a singer.

Breaking New Ground

Barbra has achieved sales unequaled by any other female recording artist. With forty-three gold albums, she is second on the all-time charts, ahead of the Beatles and the Rolling Stones and exceeded only by Elvis Presley. She has had forty-three gold and twenty-seven platinum albums, including more multiplatinum albums than all other female singers. She has earned eight Grammy awards for her work.

She continues to be the highest-selling female recording artist ever and has had number one albums in each of the last four decades. Her number one albums span a period of nearly thirty-five years, the greatest longevity in that statistic of any recording artist or group.

Timeless, Barbra's millennium New Year's Eve concert at the MGM Grand in Las Vegas, set an all-time Ticketmaster record for one-day sales of a single event, virtually selling out in the first few hours, eight months before the performance. Her Madison Square Garden concert and her Los Angeles farewell live appearances at the Staple Center had record-setting success. Barbra Streisand's 1994 concert tour also set records. The tour generated over ten million dollars for charities the artist supports, channeling money to significant causes in each location where she performed Barbra and Barry Gibb released a collaborative album, *Guilty Pleasures*, in 2005, and she stared in a comedy, *Meet the Fockers* in 2004, which marked her return to film acting following an eight-year absence from the screen.

Barbra produced pictures that spoke of causes, especially those concerning women. *Yentl*, a romantic drama with music, is about a courageous woman who discovers that nothing is impossible in matters of the heart and mind. It is a movie that celebrates women trying to fulfill their capabilities and not allowing traditional restrictions to deter them. Her follow-up film, *Nuts*, is a story about a smart woman who was shaped into an angry, antisocial character because of childhood experiences, including sexual abuse by her stepfather and neglect by her mother, who ignored the abuse out of fear of loosing her husband. Barbra's second film as a director, *The Prince of Tides*, was concerned with the consequences of childhood traumas and explored family relationships. Barbra's stories focused on love and compassion. Her stories are about positive transformation and the potential for human growth.

Her production company, Barwood Films, has placed great emphasis on bringing to television dramatic depictions of social, historic, and political issues not usually addressed in television and movies. The topics of her movies paid tribute to non-Jews who heroically saved Jews from the Holocaust. She brought a drama investigating military harassment and repression of the civil rights of gays to millions of television viewers. Her life and art are dedicated to the humanities, as reflected by the Streisand Foundation, which is committed to gaining women's equality, the protection of human rights as well as civil rights and liberties, the needs of children at risk in society, and the preservation of the environment. She is a leading spokesperson and fund-raiser for social causes close to her heart, including AIDS. Barbra Streisand is a true Renaissance woman of enormous talent, who has achieved incredible feats against all odds.

Barbra was married to Elliott Gould (her costar in Broadway's *I Can Get It for You Wholesale*) from 1963 to 1971. They have one son, Jason Gould, who appeared in *The Prince of Tides* as the awkward teenage son of Streisand's character. After well-publicized relationships with producer Jon Peters and with actors Ryan O'Neal, Don Johnson, and Liam Neeson, Streisand married actor James Brolin in 1998 in a ceremony at her home in Malibu, California.

Taught the Hard Way

Barbra learned many lessons on her journey to where she is today. She learned how to grieve, how to live in a world void of affection and imagination, and how to build a world full of fantasy, a world that motivated her and made her environment tolerable. Below is a compilation of quotations from Barbra that reflect lessons learned during her struggles.

"Myths are a waste of time. They prevent progression."

"To have ego means to believe in your own strength. And to also be open to other people's views. It is to be open, not closed. My ego is responsible for my doing what I do—bad or good."

"I just don't want to be hampered by my own limitations."

"I am simple, complex, generous, selfish, unattractive, beautiful, lazy, and driven."

"You have got to discover you, what you do, and trust it."

"I'm not that ambitious any more. I just like my privacy. I wish I really wasn't talked about at all."

"Why is it men are permitted to be obsessed about their work, but women are only permitted to be obsessed about men?"

"A human being is only interesting if he's in contact with himself."

"I learned you have to trust yourself, be what you are, and do what you ought to do the way you should do it."

And It Feels Good

The most important goal Barbra achieved was to survive the circumstances into which she had been born. She survived the death of a loving father and husband to her mother. She lived with a mother who did not have the emotional capacity to give a growing child the attention, love, and support she needed, and grandparents who did not know the meaning of affection. She endured a stepfather who had nothing but contempt for her. She learned to ignore or accept physical attributes that did not match the societal definition of beauty. Most importantly, she achieved goals most do not, including the goal of making her fantasies a reality.

5

Lessons from Little Red Riding Hood

In a great wide forest, full of beautiful trees and green glades, a long time ago there lived a woodcutter and his wife. They had only one child, a little girl. She was so pretty, and so good, that the sun seemed to shine more brightly when its light fell upon her little face, and the birds seem to sing more sweetly when she passed by.

The little girl's real name was Oprah, but the neighbors around about all called her "Little Red Riding Hood," because of a scarlet riding hood and cloak that her kind old grandmother had made for her and that she always wore.

She was a happy, merry little child, with a smile and a gentle word for everybody. Everyone loved her, and people were glad to catch a glimpse of her scarlet cloak as she tripped along, reciting poems, under the green boughs.

Little Red Riding Hood lived with her grandparents in a little white cottage with a green door and a thatched roof, and with red and white roses climbing all over the walls.

One bright spring morning early in May, when little Red Riding-Hood had just finished putting away the breakfast cups, her grandmother came bustling in from the dairy.

"Here's a to-do," she said. "Farmer Hodge has this very minute told me that he hears your great granny isn't quite well, and I can't leave the cheese-making this morning. You go, my dear, and find out how she is. Take her this little pot of sweet fresh butter, these two new-laid eggs, and these nice tasty little pasties. Maybe they'll tempt her to eat a bit. Here's your basket, and don't be too long."

So little Red Riding Hood pulled her hood over her ponytails and set off down the sunny green slope at a brisk pace, her basket in her hand. But as she got deeper into the forest, she walked more slowly. Everything was so beautiful. The great trees waved their huge arms over her, the birds called to one another from the thornbushes all white with blossoms, and the child sang as she walked.

The path wound along through the trees, and as it grew wider after turning a corner, Red Riding Hood saw that she was likely to have company on her walk. Where the two paths divided, there sat a big gray wolf, licking his long paws and looking sharply about him. "Good morning, Red Riding Hood," he said.

"Good morning, Mr. Wolf," Oprah answered.

"And where may you be going?" said Wolf, as he walked beside her.

"Oh, Great Granny isn't very well, and Grandmother cannot leave the cheese-making this morning, so I'm taking her some pastries in my basket. I am to see how she is.

"And," said Wolf, "where does Great Granny live, little lady?"

"Through the copse, and down the hollow, and over the bridge, and three meadows after the mill."

"Does she indeed?" cried he. "Why, then, I do believe she is a very dear old friend of mine, whom I have not seen for years and years. Now, I'll tell you what we'll do, you and I. I will go by this way, and you shall take that, and whoever gets there first shall be the winner of the game."

So Wolf trotted off one way, and Red Riding Hood went the other. As she crossed the last meadow from the mill, she came in sight of her great-grandmother's cottage and the big lilac bushes that grew by the garden gate.

"Oh, dear! How I must have lingered!" said Oprah, when she saw how high the sun had climbed since she set out on her journey, and, pattering up the garden path, she tapped at the cottage door.

"Who's there?" said a very gruff kind of voice from inside.

"It's only I, Great Granny dear, your little Red Riding Hood with some goodies for you in my basket," answered the little girl.

"Then pull the bobbin," cried the voice, "and the latch will go up."

"What a dreadful cold poor Great Granny must have to make her so hoarse," thought the child. Then she pulled the bobbin and the latch went up. Red Riding Hood pushed open the door and stepped inside the cottage.

It seemed very dark in there after the bright sunlight outside, and all Red Riding Hood could see was that the window curtains and the bed curtains were still drawn. Her great-grandmother seemed to be lying in bed, with the sheets pulled almost over her head and her white-frilled nightcap nearly hiding her face.

It was not her great granny at all but the wicked wolf. He had hurried to the cottage, put on Great Granny's nightcap, and popped into her bed, pretending that he was Great Granny herself.

"Come and sit down beside my bed, dearie," wheezed Wolf, "and let us have a little chat." Then the wolf stretched out his large hairy paws and began to unfasten the basket.

"Oh!" said Red Riding Hood, "what great arms you have, Great Granny!"

"All the better to hug you with," said the wolf.

"And what great rough ears you have, Great Granny!"

"All the better to hear you with, my little dear."

"And your eyes, Great Granny, what great yellow eyes you have!"

"All the better to see you with, my pet," grinned the wolf.

"And oh! Oh! Great Granny," cried the child, in a sad fright, "what great sharp teeth you have!"

"All the better to eat you with!" growled the wolf, springing up suddenly at Red Riding Hood. But just at that very moment the door flew open, and two tall woodcutters rushed in with their heavy axes and killed the wicked wolf.

"But where is Great Granny?" asked Little Red Riding Hood, when she had thanked the brave woodcutters. "Oh, where can poor Great Granny be? Could the cruel wolf have eaten her up?"

And she began to cry and sob bitterly. Just then, who should walk in but Great Granny herself, as large as life and as hearty as ever, with her market basket on her arm! There was another old woman in the village who was not very well, and Great Granny had been down to visit her to give her some of her own famous herbal tea.

So everything turned out right in the end, and all lived happily every after. But Little Red Riding Hood never made friends with a wolf again!

A happy child has a simple life, but danger could be just around the corner. If you have been taught to trust adults, you will likely do this without question, no matter who the adult is. This is dangerous because not all adults can be trusted. We have all learned not to talk to strangers. This is taught to us because we know the risk strangers can pose to children. But what about those who are not strangers? Sometimes people who are close to us can pose a greater risk.

Danger can be waiting, especially in environments you are not familiar with. When the environment changes, so do the rules and usually the people in it. You have to reevaluate how you interact and how much you can trust. This is something adults know. There is a different level of security at home than in the streets. Adults know this and adjust to the change. They do it everyday. Children, however, have not had enough experience to know that they need to adjust, or what to adjust to.

There are many caring people in the world, but there are many who are not. Bright, friendly faces with kind words offering goodies are not necessarily people you can trust. Look behind the words. What do you see? Good times may result in you being devoured.

Be careful. When you wander through the woods called life, look at the beauty but don't ignore the danger. Learn to enjoy your environment without becoming blind. And if something does not seem to be what it appears to be, it probably isn't.

6

Oprah Winfrey: Her Highness's Power

"With every experience, you alone are painting your own canvas,
thought by thought, choice by choice."
—Oprah Winfrey

Hallelujah

Oprah Gail Winfrey was born on her grandmother's family farm in Kosciusko,
Mississippi. Her father, Vernon Winfrey, twenty-one years of age, was a soldier.
Her mother, Vernita Lee, was an eighteen-year-old housemaid. Her parents never
married. Oprah was an unplanned pregnancy. Her mother knew that staying in
the South and trying to raise Oprah was not what she wanted. Shortly after

Oprah's birth, Vernita left Mississippi and headed to the North, where she felt she would have a better chance to put her life together. Her future was not in Mississippi, even though she would have to leave her baby there. In search of a new life, Vernita found work as a housemaid in Milwaukee, Wisconsin.

Vernita left Oprah behind in the care of her grandmother, Hattie Mae Lee, when she moved to Milwaukee. Oprah's father, Vernon, would not be a part of her life until later. Vernita's goal of making a life for herself, up North, was her focus. Oprah would spend six years with her grandmother.

Oprah was raised on Hattie Mae's small farm. This was a blessing. Oprah was isolated from the bustle of a city and all the hardships that come with it. Her grandmother was a kind woman. She gave Oprah the attention and affection all children need to grow into healthy, happy people.

Oprah's time with her grandmother helped her to develop talents and values she would rely on later in her life. While living with her grandmother, she learned to read at a very early age, before she started preschool, instilling a love of reading she retains today. Oprah would read whatever was available and developed extraordinary oratory skills, especially for someone her age. Reading was one of Oprah's favorite pastimes as there wasn't much else to do on the farm.

Oprah's grandmother's strong religious beliefs geared Oprah toward attending church regularly. Oprah was very active in the church. She loved to recite for the congregation. This was the beginning of her public-speaking career, reading aloud and reciting sermons for the congregation of her church. By the time she was three, she had traveled through the South, reciting sermons and biblical verses. Her speaking career was on its way.

As safe and peaceful as the farm was, Oprah's childhood was anything but glamorous. They had an outhouse, which forced Oprah to use a slop jar, kept in the bedroom, for a toilet at night. Oprah did not have a room of her own. She slept with her grandmother, while her grandfather slept in a separate room. Her days were filled with chores and were without playmates, television, or toys. She used a corncob for a doll and rode one of the pigs bareback for entertainment and fun. She was a curious child. Her only friends were farm animals, and she made the best of them. She gave the animals parts in the plays she created and included them in games. Her directing and producing career had begun. As a child, Oprah never wasted a minute of her young, imaginative mind. She made her environment interesting.

Oprah was told again and again by her grandmother that she was gifted and special. Oprah believed that someday she would do incredible things. Holding on to that belief saved her. It gave her the drive to become more than what her environment offered her. The praise helped her through the hard years she would encounter in the future.

Oprah was too young to know the meaning of special and unique. She didn't know how accurate her grandmother was in describing her as special. She only knew how good it made her feel, and that it was a good thing. Knowing that her mother had left her behind made Oprah feel unloved and unwanted. Her grandmother made up for this by giving Oprah a sense of her own value.

Oprah's talent for reading and presenting herself to an audience opened the door to all types of possibilities. Today, Oprah is grateful for the life her grandmother gave her. In those days, there were many young black children in the South who were born to unwed parents. Some stayed with parents who struggled. In Oprah's case, her mother decided to do her struggling alone. This may have appeared to be a selfish act, but no one but Vernita knows why she did it. Was it for her child's sake or for her own benefit? Whatever the reason, she left Oprah in a better environment than she, her mother, could offer her.

Even though it was lonely on the farm, the environment had its positive attributes. Early environmental factors have a strong influence on young children. The basic foundation on which Oprah was to build her future lay in those early years. Although she was poor in so many ways, she didn't lack a sense of safety or security. Oprah would have developed into a totally different person had her mother chosen to take her up North with her from the start. The morals and values she learned from her grandmother gave Oprah the foundation she needed to steady herself later in her life. She might not have had the success she has today without this foundation, much of which was rooted in her love of reading and performing for an audience.

On Sundays, Oprah would dress up in her best clothes and go to the Buffalo United Methodist Church with her grandmother. It was at this church that Oprah first spoke in public. Her first recital was at Easter. She went on to recite verses and poems at churches in neighboring cities. The women in the church would remark on how gifted she was. By the time she was four, the entire town in which she lived knew she was gifted.

Church was a very important part of her life as a child. She used every chance she had to perform in front of an audience, never missing an opportunity to recite biblical verses. Everyone was astonished by how articulate young Winfrey was. She felt proud seeing her name on the church program. She took the pride and attention she gained from church as a sign that she would someday be that special person everyone thought she would be.

Oprah perceived herself as someone who had a special gift. She knew it was a gift because of the reaction she received from others. She felt like a special and loved person because of the attention she received. The belief that she could get love from this talent was a belief that would keep her struggling for perfection throughout her life.

When Oprah entered kindergarten, the teachers decided she was too advanced and moved her into the first grade. Her grandmother was very proud of this accomplishment. Grandma had instilled an important mixture of education and discipline in Oprah.

Young Oprah had a goal that was vague in nature. She didn't know what she wanted to accomplish, but knew that she wanted her life to be better than it was. The farm, as comfortable as it may have been in between the chores, could not satisfy the taste of someone who was so hungry for excitement. Her wish for a better life was strong, so strong that she could feel it around her and knew that someday she would be living it

Oprah remembers standing on the back, screened-in porch with her grandmother while her grandmother was boiling clothes. It was a hard life on the farm; everyone had chores, no matter the age, no matter the gender. She watched day after day as her grandmother worked the farm. Oprah was determined that her life would not consist of this. Not that she was shy about hard work, but the type of work she wanted would not be found in a pot. She admired her grandparents' work, though, and she would model her own work ethic after them.

Oprah wasn't popular with the children in her church's congregation. Her popularity with the adults did not rub off on their children; instead, it spawned jealousy. The appreciation Oprah received from the adults caused her to receive rejection from her peers. Some literally would spit on her. They saw her as a show-off. But she had a natural talent she needed to express, and she would continue to express this talent throughout her life.

Will Someone Spare Some Love?

When Oprah was six, her mother decided it was time for her to come to Milwaukee and live with her. Oprah's mother, Vernita, had a job as a maid and felt that she could now raise her daughter. Her hopes were not based on her ability alone. She expected her boyfriend to help her. She thought they would be a family. Her boyfriend had promised to marry her and move Oprah and her into a new house. After Oprah arrived, the boyfriend did not follow through on his promise. Instead, Oprah and her mother lived in one room in another woman's home.

During this time, Vernita became pregnant and gave birth to Oprah's sister, Patricia. Vernita thought that the birth of this child would increase the probability that her boyfriend would marry her and help her provide a better life for her and her children. It did not. Now there were three of them living in one room. This was a difficult adjustment for Oprah. She was used to the space and freedom of a farm. Now she was cramped into one room with her mother and her baby sister. She missed those days on the farm with her grandmother.

The moralistic and loving values she saw displayed by her grandmother were not in her mother. Vernita's focus was on getting a husband. She thought this would solve all her problems. She had numerous love affairs, none of which worked out. Oprah continually saw her mother in romantic situations that were anything but romantic. She saw her mother used by one man after another.

Oprah's country living had given way to the rules of the ghetto where they lived. Oprah began to have difficulties with her sister. There was intense sibling rivalry. Two years later, her mother had a baby boy. The father of her brother did not marry her mother either. Vernita now had three children to care for. She was barely able to take care of one. Oprah had not been getting enough attention before the birth of her siblings; now, with the arrival of an infant brother, the attention she received deceased. Oprah fought with her brother and sister to get attention. She began telling lies to get what she wanted.

Her mother couldn't take on the responsibility of three children. She felt Oprah was the most difficult and, as she had years before, felt that she would not be able to raise Oprah. This was not only because Oprah was trouble, but because now she had other children who were much younger to care for. She sent Oprah to Nashville to live with her father when she was nine years old.

Her father and his wife enjoyed having Oprah live with them. She filled the void of a childless home and was a delight to have around. The happiness shared at her new home was to be short-lived. Not long after her arrival in Nashville, Oprah's mother, feeling that she could handle all her children, sent for Oprah to come back to Milwaukee to live with her.

Oprah was confused. This was her third move. There was no stability in her young life. There was no predictability. Oprah never knew what would happen next. Lack of a stable home and the inability to predict what will happen next can make an individual insecure. Children have little control over their environment and therefore rely on familiarity and routine to feel some measure of order and security. Oprah had none of this in her life.

Oprah returned to her mother. Things had not changed much. They lived in poverty and her mother worked all the time. Oprah was not receiving the attention she had been accustomed to in Nashville with her father and stepmother. So Oprah looked elsewhere for security and a sense of belonging.

Oprah turned to family members and friends of the family for the support she could not get from her mother. It would be these individuals, to whom she turned for security, who would victimize her. Her mother proved to be unable to support her and rescue her from these predators.

When Oprah was nine, her nineteen-year-old cousin, who was her babysitter, sexually abused her. This was a painful and confusing time for Oprah. She was told by her cousin to keep their sexual encounters quiet; she was not to tell anyone about what had happened. Oprah remembers not telling anyone because she thought she would be blamed for it. In situations such as this, individuals blame themselves thinking there must be something wrong with them.

This confusion was partly the result of the way her cousin acted afterward. Her cousin took her to the zoo and gave her ice cream, asking her to swear to be silent. The abuse did not stop there. Oprah was raped by her cousin, a family friend, her mother's live-in boyfriend, and her favorite uncle. Each of the four told her that if she ever told, they would both be in a lot of trouble.

Often children will keep sexual abuse a secret because they don't have the language to describe it, or they don't think anyone will believe them. Childhood victims are often frightened into keeping the secret by the perpetrators, who may have threatened to harm them or those dear to them if they tell anyone about what had happened. Children often hesitate to disclose what has happened to them because it would come down to taking the word of the adult against the word of the child.

A child feels vulnerable with an adult under normal situations. Situations in which there is secrecy and threats made by multiple adults will make a child keep a secret he or she wants to disclose. The child has seen from other examples that the one with the most power wins. The adult wins in the end.

Telling about the abuse can have serious negative consequences, including the breakup of the family. Once a child has told, the child begins to question whether he or she should have broken the silence. Children who tell often observe the negative consequences and feel significant pressure to recant their story. Many children believe that they are somehow at least partially to blame for the abuse and, because of the shame and guilt associated with it, will not come forward.

Another reason why people who are victims of sexual abuse don't come forward is because of what they are told about their contribution to the act. Sexual assault, including rape is a criminal offense. One is violated emotionally and physically. This is done without one's consent or one's ability to give consent, especially if the victim is a child. Children cannot give adults consent to perform any sexual behavior or act.

There are myths that place the responsibility on the victim and not on the perpetrator, making it difficult to disclose the event. This applies to children as well as adults. Some of these myths are

- If someone doesn't try hard enough to get away, they are not sexually abused.
- The victim asked for it and enjoyed it.
- If they did not ask for it, they deserved it by their behavior.
- Females have fantasies about being raped.
- Sexual assault only happens among strangers.
- If the abuse doesn't physically hurt them, they'll get over it.

Oprah wasn't given any support or treatment during or immediately after each abuse. Treatment cannot begin for victimized children until someone learns that the abuse took place. Oprah told no one, and, of course, none of the perpetrators volunteered any information. Perpetrators almost never disclose their acts voluntarily. If disclosure takes place at all, it is the victim who communicates what happened. Abuse victims often do not tell, and those who do tell usually wait a very long time. Survivors of trauma, like those sexually abused by trusted loved ones, frequently require a lot of time to come to an understanding about what happened to them, and only then can they communicate it. The information must come out slowly and be paced; otherwise, they often are overwhelmed by it.

The sexual abuse Oprah experienced was not her only problem. The shame and guilt she felt because of the abuse caused her to act out. Children often do not know how to dispel the anger they feel toward themselves or others. As articulate as Oprah was, this was one story that she could not articulate properly. Even if she could have, she didn't want to. So she screamed out by acting out. Acting out for children often includes running away, being confrontational and oppositional, becoming sexually promiscuous, stealing, and doing a variety of self-destructive or demeaning acts toward themselves and others. Her acting out touched every part of her life. Oprah's wildness was not confined to home. She stayed out late, sometimes for the whole night, with men older than herself.

Oprah desperately wanted love from her mother, who was too busy working and tending to her own life. The bonding between them never took place. Not getting the attention she needed from her mother made her seek it in other places, usually with men. She became their sex toy. These men were not strangers; they were family members and their friends. When Oprah was thirteen years old, young men would come over to her house. Oprah would get rid of her brother by giving him ice cream or candy and sending him outside to play. She would then do "the horse" with these men. The men were nineteen or twenty years old.

Oprah began running away, hanging out with the wrong crowd, chasing after anything male. She gave the boys what they wanted in exchange for what she wanted but would never get: love and belongingness. Oprah was not sure who knew what was happening, and no one tried to stop it. Oprah liked the sexual attention she got from men and boys, and this behavior went on for some time.

One of the men who sexually abused her was her favorite uncle, whom she admired. She was fourteen when he molested her. One day when they were alone, he took her panties off and penetrated her with his fingers. This incestuous affair continued for some time. Oprah later told her father and stepmother, but her uncle claims that it is a lie (Mair, 20).

Usually sexual assault of a child involves a slow conditioning process where the level and type of sexual abuse increases over time. Incest victims are conditioned into submitting and displaying affection. The affection then gradually becomes more sexual with time. A child like Oprah, who sought approval and affection from the adults in her life, was deprived of a chance to learn to distinguish between the physical affection that is sexually exploitative and the normal affection displayed by those who care. In this situation, a child's confusion may be heightened by her or his own feelings of shame and guilt, often cultivated by the abuser.

For many years, incest and other childhood sexual abuse has been covered up by silence. An offender uses real or implied force, or exploits the child's natural desire for love and attention. The child submits out of fear and/or the desire to be loved and cared for because she or he is not in a position of power.

How might this apply to you or someone you know? There are certain signs that point toward sexual abuse or the setting up of such abuse. Some of these are being touched in a way that makes you feel uncomfortable, being fondled without your permission, or being kissed in a way that is inappropriate for the relationship. It includes someone showing pornographic pictures and telling sexual stories, or someone touching himself or herself in a sexual manner in front of you or forcing you to share an intimate space such as a bed when it was not necessary.

These are important behaviors to recognize, identify, and disclose in order to stop the sexual abuse.

Adult survivors, once physically free from the sexual abuse of childhood, often continue to be silent. Oprah kept silent until she was in a safe place, living with her father. She would later be outed publicly to the tabloids by her sister. When Oprah was being abused, she was in a position where there was no support. She may have felt that if she told, she would destroy what little family she had. Many times the revelation that sexual abuse has happened in the family will destroy the impression of a healthy, caring family. The family, feeling threatened, will refuse to discuss the abuse. This decreases the victim's ability to cope in a healthy way. Later, when Oprah was living with her father, where she felt safe and there was support, she told of the abuse.

Oprah found ways to cope. She was reading, learning, and excelling in school. She became unpopular with her peers again because of her academic achievements. The school she attended was not the type of school where academics took precedence over socializing and hanging out. Not being accepted by her peers was hard for Oprah. She wanted so much to be accepted and loved. Her peers' rejection was extreme, and sometimes people would threaten to beat her up. At age thirteen, Oprah won a scholarship to a program called Upward Bound. This allowed Oprah to attend an all-white school in an expensive Milwaukee suburb where academic excellence was valued. She was the only black student in her school.

This opportunity caused an additional problem, since Oprah began comparing herself to the classmates in her new school. Not only was Oprah's mother not like those of her affluent classmates, but her lifestyle was different. Oprah could not afford to keep up with her classmates from affluent white homes, so she stole from her mother. She faked home robberies to account for the missing items she had taken. She became a thief to make up for the difference between her lifestyle and that of her classmates. She felt she had to do this in order to keep up with her peers.

Oprah wanted a mother who could spend time with her. She wanted a lifestyle like that of her classmates. She wanted the love and emotional support she needed. Oprah knew her mother was not like the other mothers, and this added to her frustration and hurt. Why couldn't she have a mother like the girls at her school? She wanted a mother who would be attentive to her needs. But Oprah knew that her mother was more like the maids who took the bus with her in the morning. She knew her mother was just trying to survive. Her way of showing love to Oprah was getting up and going to work every day, in order to feed and clothe the family.

Oprah's reading was a healing tool for her. She read *A Tree Grows in Brooklyn*, then Maya Angelou's *I Know Why the Caged Bird Sings*. These books helped Oprah gain insight into her abuse. She had never known, heard, or read about anyone who had suffered from sexual abuse. She read these books and could identify with the pain and sorrow these women had gone through, because it was also her pain and sorrow. When she read *The Color Purple*, it moved her. She had to put the book down after reading the first page and cry. She could not believe that someone actually put such experiences in writing. It was an important part of the healing process for her because all this time she had carried the burden of being abused alone, believing that no one else had experienced it. It made her feel as though she was not so bad after all.

She had lived a lot by her fourteenth birthday. She had been and was going through sexual abuse, had moved to a different city three times, and had begun running away from home. She hated living where she lived and the life she was leading.

Once when she was fourteen, she ran away from home for a week. She came home when she ran out of money and called the family minister, asking him to help smooth over the situation with her mother. Oprah had become a sexually promiscuous teenager, one who got into a lot of trouble. She took total responsibility for what had happened to her. She thought little of herself and had no way of breaking away from the self-destructive path down which she had started.

Oprah's problems increased. Her mother didn't know what to do with her. Her mother tried to send her to a girls' detention home. Fortunately for Oprah, she was denied admission to the home because there were no openings at that time, but officials at the home told them she might be admitted in two weeks. Despite the poor decisions her mother had made in the past, she was about to make a decision which would change Oprah's life for the better. So in what may have been her second major stroke of good luck, instead of going to the detention home, once again Oprah was sent to live with her father in Nashville.

Unknowingly Oprah would carry a problem caused by her promiscuous behavior in Milwaukee to Nashville with her. When she arrived in Nashville, she gave birth to a stillborn baby boy. She was only fourteen and had been hiding her condition in shame. After her miscarriage, Oprah began naming all of the men she had sex with, including her uncle Trent. The death of her baby devastated her, and she vowed to turn her life around.

Her sexual activities were her greatest shame. She told her father about her sexual encounters as a teen, but revealed it to no one else. After she had left her father's home, graduated from high school and college, and built a successful career on the Oprah Winfrey show this information became public when her sister revealed it to a tabloid. When this happened, Oprah was stunned, so stunned that she became sick and was bedridden, believing that the world would hate her for what she had done. It would take two years before she would speak to her sister again.

A decision to tell people about sexual abuse or to confront a perpetrator can be healing. However, coming to terms with what happened long ago can be threatening because it may result in rearranging how one views the world, especially one's own world. The stakes are high. On the other hand, going public or confronting a perpetrator can, for the first time, empower the victim.

There are many ways people experience the harm resulting from having been sexually abused. When an individual discloses sexual abuse to a family member, a supportive response is not necessarily what the person will receive. In fact, it is usually not the first response. People who are informed can be supportive or rejecting, may believe or disbelieve, may take the disclosure seriously or pretend not to hear it.

Unfortunately, concern for the family often outweighs concerns for the affected individual. The most hurtful comment that relatives frequently make to older victims of childhood sexual abuse is "it happened such a long time ago, just get over it." Like scar tissue, the effects of sexual abuse never go away. They continue to influence victims in various ways, and may lead to drug and alcohol abuse, low self-esteem, divorce, and distrust. When a family member sexually abuses a child, the effects can be particularly devastating: a trusted person suddenly does something that feels terribly wrong.

Sexual abuse can forever alter a person's view of the world. A person is likely to be left with strong feelings of anger, fear, shame, hurt, and disappointment. Girls are more likely to act out against themselves, perhaps developing emotional problems. Boys often act out against others, sometimes becoming perpetrators of abuse themselves.

Although each person responds in his or her own way to the experience of incest or sexual abuse, research indicates that there are many common issues, especially among women with such a history.

Sexual abuse affects one's self esteem. It leaves the person feeling that she or he is not a worthwhile person. Abused individuals feel bad, dirty, and/or ashamed and can become self-destructive or suicidal. They are confused as to what they feel. They become afraid of their feelings because their feelings have led to painful experiences in the past. They experience a narrow range of feelings, blocking themselves off from many feelings to protect themselves from emotional pain. They experience intrusive memories, images, and nightmares, often reliving past traumatic events. They experience increased anger or irritability. Sexual abuse victims have difficulty with intimacy. They find it difficult to trust others and have trouble making a commitment, experiencing panic when people get too close.

Often the shame, guilt, and pain that women experience as a result of incest are found hidden in substance abuse or other destructive behaviors, such as promiscuity or eating disorders. Many women experience actual physical symptoms that can become debilitating over time.

People cope with sexual abuse in different ways. Oprah coped by becoming a superachiever. This gave her back the control she felt she had lost.

Not on My Watch

This was the second time Oprah had lived with her father, Vernon, and stepmother, Zelma. Her mother sent her to live with them for a short while when Oprah was nine years old. Zelma and Vernon received a different Oprah at age fourteen then they had at age nine. A lot had happened in those years. Oprah had had experiences children should not go through. Oprah had lived a life of a woman on the streets. She had experienced the worse of adult life while still in a child's body and with an inexperienced mind. But she was not the sum of her experiences. She knew this, and so did her father and stepmother.

She was now in a strict home. Chaste behavior and high grades were demanded. This was something Oprah had to get used to. She did not resist parental guidance. Her lack of resistance was probably because that, along with the demands, she also received attention and love. It was clear that their rules were for her own good, whether she liked it or not.

Oprah's years with her father were marked by Vernon's strong hand and Zelma's steady support. They instilled discipline and the value of hard work. They gave her a real home, something she had not had since leaving them years earlier. Oprah's mother had done the right thing sending her to live with her father. She was sent to Nashville for the purpose of straightening her out. It was her mother's way of rescuing her daughter.

And so Vernon did. No daughter of his was going to be cheap and slutty. She would be a picture of integrity and class. And so the work started and the change began. She started wearing conservative high-school clothes. She dressed, talked, and acted like a young lady of breeding. Oprah became what her father hoped she would be.

Oprah had to change her ways. The coping skills she had adopted in Milwaukee would not be tolerated here. Running to older men for comfort in the form of sexual acts, running away from home when things did not go her way, stealing, truancy, and most of all self-degradation in the name of self-pity would not take place in this home.

The healing process would be long and constant for Oprah. This process is both painful and hard. The hardest part of the healing process is letting go of survival techniques that helped a victim stay alive and sane during a period of childhood sexual abuse. However, once older and safe, former victims need to learn to let go of those parts of their behavior that are destructive and inappropriate. Once out of danger, these coping techniques no longer help but rather keep the survivor from forming close, trusting relationships with caring people.

Vernon wanted nothing but the best from his daughter. He knew her potential was great, and he expected her to achieve it. He made sure that his daughter stuck to her curfew and maintained high grades in school. Oprah's father was a crucial factor in her turning her life around. Oprah knew that in Nashville she had to obey her father and stepmother. She was made to read five books every two weeks and follow a new set of rules. She had a twelve o'clock curfew, which was different from her all-nighters in Milwaukee.

Oprah's father would not tolerate Cs from her. He had a lot of faith in his daughter's ability and knew she was not a C student. He wanted her to be the best she could be. He did not feel he was pushing her too hard or insisting that she be something that she was not. He wanted to motivate her to do her best and felt that setting high standards would help her to achieve this goal. Oprah met that standard; she knew nothing else would be acceptable.

When she was living with her mother, everything was acceptable, not because her mother was accepting of it but because there was no monitoring of what Oprah did. She got away with behavior that would not be tolerated in most homes. When she moved into her father's home, she knew that she could not think of such behavior, much less act on it. She never tried to get away with inappropriate behavior in her father's home. Oprah needed structure and the right type of attention, which is what she received.

Oprah began dating in high school, the type of dating common to girls her age. She never had sex with her high school boyfriend, Anthony. She now viewed her body as something of value, which should not be given out to everyone. This was a new stance. She was not starving for attention and love; she was receiving that at home. She wanted a healthy, normal teenage relationship.

She avoided speaking of her mother to her boyfriend. She never spoke of her mother, siblings, or her life in Milwaukee. These were memories she wanted to leave behind. Carrying the past into a relationship would color her relationship in ways that would not be beneficial for her or her boyfriend. Sometimes it's the knowledge that people have of your past experiences that keeps you from letting go and moving on. You may know that you are not the sum of these experiences, but it is hard to convince others of that. To her boyfriend, she was the new girl who looked and acted properly, a girl with an exciting personality. They met at a community dance, and their meeting was the beginning of a freshly defined course of intimacy for Oprah.

Oprah had a good relationship with her boyfriend and was not sorry she was keeping her past a secret. Her boyfriend and schoolmates saw a girl who was together in every way. There was no need to question her past; they could see what she was made of. She was getting what she needed from family and friends now. Her current life seemed so different from her past, which had been anything but supportive. It was the kind of past that severely dysfunctional, maladjusted children come from—not an Oprah. It was the kind of past that causes children to run away and support themselves by any means possible, so that they could get away from the hell they live in.

Yes, Oprah had dealt with her past, but there was still shame and guilt associated with it. It was not the kind of information she wanted people to know about her. She wanted to leave it in the past, so she buried it deep inside. One day, however, it would surface in an unexpected way. She was able to keep her past indiscretions from her friends, but she knew what had happened and the scars were still there. She had scars that did not show on the surface, but damage had been done.

It was incredible that she was able to develop an intimate relationship with a male and not carry her past relationships into her first real romantic connection. Her father provided a good example of what she should look for in a man. He was a man who felt that a woman should be smart and disciplined, and most of all a lady. She took clues from him on how a man should act toward a lady, with respect and admiration.

Sex was not in the picture for her. This was a real test as to how her past sexual abuse would affect her ability to be intimate. The most tragic aftereffect of incest is the enormous difficulty survivors often have in trusting others and in forming satisfying intimate, loving relationships. They have difficulty seeing themselves as anything but sex objects and seeing their intimates as anything but users or abusers.

She handled herself well and reveled in being able to be a normal teenager. She had a good time engaging in the type of activities people her age should engage in. Both she and her boyfriend were interested in school, both in academics and in extracurricular activities. It was nice for her to have someone who was interested in doing things with her instead of doing things to her. Oprah was learning a new world of socialization, not only with her boyfriend but with her schoolmates, who were accepting of her. She was finally favored among her peers and felt she belonged.

Oprah was one of the first blacks admitted to East Nashville High School. This was the perfect place for her to grow. She enrolled in drama classes and was active in student politics. She became student council president. At seventeen, she was invited to a White House conference on youth and represented East Nashville at a national speaking competition. Her talent in speaking was paying off. Something she had started at age three, before she entered school, was opening doors for her in her teens.

She was well liked by the students and teachers. They were not intimidated by her intelligence and gifts. She spoke to churches and women's groups whenever possible. To further develop her talent, Oprah signed up for public speaking at school. Oprah was busy. She participated in the production of a radio show and competed in pageants, where she impressed judges and mesmerized crowds with her public-speaking talent. She loved performing and having the attention of an audience.

She was enjoying her new school; it seemed to fit her. She was motivated in all the right ways and was receiving the kind of attention appropriate for a girl her age: attention based on her personality and intelligence. She was full of energy, and that energy radiated out to others. Oprah had found her place and was excelling at being herself. She did not have to work at trying to get attention from people who did not care about her welfare. She was doing what she enjoyed and was receiving positive attention for it.

It seemed so long ago, that world of men, running away, stealing, and staying out all night. It seemed so far away that Oprah forgot it existed. But it was a part of her that had not been completely resolved, and it would push to the surface when she let her guard down.

When Oprah was a senior in high school, a local radio station observed her drama class rehearsing. WVOL asked Oprah if she'd like to read on the radio. They gave her a job reading the news. Oprah then entered a public-speaking contest. The prize was a scholarship to Tennessee State University (TSU). She won the scholarship and enrolled in speech communications and performing arts. She worked at the radio station and studied at night.

During her freshman year at TSU, Oprah won several pageants, including "Miss Black Nashville" and "Miss Tennessee." She was the image of perfection, beauty, strength, and intelligence. She was special, just as her grandmother had told her in her youth, and she was a lady, just as her father demanded of her in her teen years. She was sparking interest everywhere and was spotted by a local television show. They saw the uniqueness and quality in this young woman. The local CBS television station offered her a job as a coanchor.

And So I Spoke and They Listened

Oprah had learned early on that she had a gift, and that her gift of speech and ability to connect with others would offer her the world she wanted. Oprah can remember standing on her grandmother's porch and thinking, not out of shame but out of determination, how her life wouldn't be like this. She wanted her life to be better. Oprah looks back on how strict her father was and loves him for it. She says he was a big influence in her life. He always wanted Oprah to make the best of her life, and he wouldn't accept anything less than her best (Mair, 24).

Oprah believes today that you must be true to yourself. Honesty comes from your natural instinct telling you when you are doing something that fits your values. When you accomplish something and it feels right, you feel a sense of accomplishment, fulfillment, and worthiness in the world, in such a way that you know that you are doing the right thing. You don't have to ask anyone. You don't need the approval of others to feel secure in your decision. You know its right because it feels right on every level.

Oprah was ready to be true to herself and to take the next step. This meant leaving the security of her father's home and looking for work outside of Nashville. A few months before she graduated from Tennessee State University, she was offered a full-time job as a reporter in Baltimore, Maryland. She had to decide between the job and staying in school to graduate. She chose the job because it presented such a great opportunity.

As a reporter, Oprah found it hard to hide what she felt. She would cry during sad stories and laugh at the funny ones. She did not do well as a reporter. She was better as a news coanchor in Baltimore, working at WJZ-TV news. In 1978, she became cohost of WJZ-TV's *People Are Talking*, a morning talk show, while continuing to serve as coanchor for news shows. After the first talk show, Oprah knew that this was what she wanted to do. It was a place and a job where she could be herself. Oprah helped make the show popular.

In 1981, Oprah sent her *People Are Talking* tapes to a talk show in Chicago called *AM Chicago* and was immediately offered a job. In January 1984, she came to Chicago to host WLS-TV's *AM Chicago*. The show was having a lot of difficulties and was not rated as high as had been hoped. She turned the show into a hit in less than a year. It was a half-hour show when she began. The format was soon expanded to one hour, and in September 1985, it was renamed *The Oprah Winfrey Show*.

Cruise Control

On September 8, 1986, *The Oprah Winfrey Show* was first broadcast nationally. In June 1987, it won three Daytime Emmy awards for outstanding direction, outstanding host, and outstanding talk/service program. The following year, the show won a Daytime Emmy award as the outstanding talk/service program.

The Oprah Winfrey Show became the number one talk show in national syndication in less than a year after its first national broadcast. In June 1988, *The Oprah Winfrey Show* received its second consecutive Daytime Emmy award as the outstanding talk/service program. Oprah also received the International Radio and Television Society's Broadcaster of the Year award. She was the youngest person and only the fifth woman ever to receive the honor in IRTS's twenty-five-year history.

In addition to her television career, Oprah acted in movies. In 1985, she captured the nation's attention with her portrayal of Sofia in Steven Spielberg's adaptation of Alice Walker's novel, *The Color Purple*. Oprah's performance earned her nominations for an Oscar and a Golden Globe in the category of best supporting actress. Critics again applauded her performance in *Native Son*, a film adaptation of Richard Wright's classic 1940 novel.

Her love of acting and her desire to bring quality entertainment to the public prompted her to form her own production company, HARPO Productions Inc. in 1986. Based in Chicago, HARPO Entertainment Group includes HARPO Productions Inc., HARPO Films, and HARPO Video Inc. In October 1988, HARPO Productions Inc. acquired ownership and all production responsibilities for *The Oprah Winfrey Show* from Capitol Cities/ABC, making Oprah Winfrey the first woman in history to own and produce her own talk show. The following year, HARPO produced its first television miniseries, *The Women of Brewster Place*, with Oprah Winfrey as star and executive producer. This show was followed by the TV movies *There Are No Children Here* (1993) and *Before Women Had Wings* (1997), which she both produced and appeared in. In 1998, she starred in the feature film *Beloved*, from the book by the Nobel Prize—winning American author, Toni Morrison. Oprah Winfrey stands as a beacon. She has a personal fortune estimated at more than a billion dollars. She owns her own production company, which creates feature films, primetime TV specials, and home videos.

In 1991, motivated by her memories of childhood abuse, Oprah initiated a campaign to establish a national database of convicted child abusers, and she testified before the U.S. Senate Judiciary Committee on behalf of a National Child Protection Act. President Clinton signed the "Oprah Bill" into law in 1993, establishing the national database she had sought, which is now available to law enforcement agencies and concerned parties across the country.

In 2005, Oprah Winfrey was named one of the one hundred most influential people of the twentieth century by *Time* magazine, and in 1998, she received a Lifetime Achievement award from the National Academy of Television Arts and Sciences. Her influence extended to the publishing industry when she began an on-the-air book club. Oprah's Book Club selections became instant best sellers, and in 1999 she was presented with the National Book Foundation's fiftieth anniversary gold medal for her service to books and authors.

She is one of the partners in Oxygen Media Inc., a cable channel and interactive network presenting programming designed primarily for women. In 2000, Oprah's Angel Network began presenting a $100,000 "Use Your Life Award" to people who are using their lives to improve the lives of others. When *Forbes* magazine published its list of America's billionaires for the year 2003, it disclosed that Oprah Winfrey was the first African American woman to become a billionaire. In 2005, she was named by *Forbes* as one of the ten most powerful women in the world.

But it is through her talk show that her influence has been greatest. *The Oprah Winfrey Show* has an estimated daily audience of fourteen million in the United States and millions more in 132 other countries. Any book she chooses for her on-the-air book club becomes an instant best seller. When she established the "world's largest piggy bank," people all over the country contributed spare change to raise more than $81 million, which was matched by Oprah, to send disadvantaged kids to college. When she blurted that hearing about the threat of mad cow disease "just stopped me cold from eating another burger!" the perceived threat to the beef industry was enough to trigger a multimillion-dollar lawsuit.

Trial by Fire

Oprah learned a lot from her experiences. She has had a life filled with pain, which tested a young child and adolescent in the cruelest way. Her lessons were not learned in a book but lived through a life that has been as dramatic as the movies in which she would later star. Her experiences could have broken her, but instead she held on for the ride and learned. She learned lessons to share. The following are some of those lessons.

"It doesn't matter who you are, where you come from. The ability to triumph begins with you. Always."

"Lots of people want to ride with you in the limo, but what you want is someone who will take the bus with you when the limo breaks down."

"I have a lot of things to prove to myself. One is that I can live my life fearlessly."

"Your true passion should feel like breathing; it's that natural."

"My philosophy is that not only are you responsible for your life, but doing the best at this moment puts you in the best place for the next moment."

"Become the change you want to see—those are words I live by."

"Cheers to a new year and another chance for us to get it right."

"I define joy as a sustained sense of well-being and internal peace—a connection to what matters."

"I know for sure that what we dwell on is who we become."

"I trust that everything happens for a reason, even when we're not wise enough to see it."

"If you want your life to be more rewarding, you have to change the way you think."

"Understand that the right to choose your own path is a sacred privilege. Use it. Dwell in possibility."

"We are each responsible for our own life—no other person is or even can be."

"Whatever you fear most has no power—it is your fear that has the power."

"Energy is the essence of life. Every day you decide how you're going to use it by knowing what you want and what it takes to reach that goal, and by maintaining focus."

"Most all the mistakes I've made in my life, I've made because I was trying to please other people."

And So I Was Special

Oprah had a difficult task overcoming the obstacles that stood in her way. She started out by being abandoned by her parents, yet she would later spend her first years with a grandmother who would give her her greatest attribute and source of strength. She had her dignity and security stripped away from her by the people who should have protected her. She had to survive by selling herself to the lowest bidders, who cared no more about her than they would have cared about a toy that could be played with and tossed into a corner. Despite the things she had to endure during her adolescent years, she managed to hold on to her grandmother's gift, tucking it away and keeping it pure. She retrieved it when it was safe to pull out, in her father's care. There she held onto the goal of becoming the best person she could be, and that she did.

Oprah held on to what she had learned at her grandmother's farm as a young child: that she was special and would achieve great things.

7

Falling with Alice in Wonderland

Young Alice (also know as Drew) sits by the riverbank, feeling bored. Suddenly, a white rabbit scampers back, proclaims that it is very late, and pulls a pocket watch out of its waistcoat. Drew becomes very interested. She follows the rabbit, hopping right down a deep rabbit hole after him, giving no thought of how she plans to get out again.

She seems to fall quite slowly, having time to observe the things around her. She seems to fall for an interminable amount of time and begins to worry that she might fall straight through to the other side of the earth. Finally, she reaches the bottom of the hole. She is in a long hallway, and she is just in time to see the white rabbit hurrying away.

The hallway is lined with doors, but all of them are locked. On a three-legged table made of glass, Drew finds a key, but it is far too small for any of the locks. Then, Drew finds a tiny door hidden behind a curtain. The key works, but the door is far too small. Drew goes back to the table, where a little bottle has appeared. The label says "DRINK ME," and after checking to see if the bottle is marked "poison," Drew drinks it all. She shrinks to a size small enough to go through the door, but she soon realizes that she has left the key on top of the glass table. She is now too short to reach it. Seeing her dilemma and feeling foolish for her mistake, she begins to cry. But she then finds a piece of cake, on which is a little slip of paper that says "EAT ME." Drew eats, and then waits for the results.

As the cake takes effect, Drew finds herself growing larger. This time, she keeps growing until she is the size of a giant. Now, getting through the door will be more difficult than ever, and Drew begins to cry.

Suddenly Drew realizes that she has put on the rabbit's gloves. If they fit, she must be shrinking again. She soon slips and falls into a vast body of salt water. It is the pool of tears that she cried when she was a giant. Drew's size changes.

She enters the house. In the house, she finds gloves and a tiny bottle, similar to the one she drank from before. There is no sign instructing her to drink, but she begins to drink anyway. Suddenly, she grows so large that she can barely fit in the house. There is no apparent way out.

As she sits in the house, she sees a group of tiny animals standing outside. They don't appear to want to help. The animals and Drew are at a standoff. When she hears them planning to set the house on fire, she calls out that they'd better not. Before long, they launch a barrowful of little pebbles in through a window, some of which hit Drew in the face. But after they land, the pebbles turn into little cakes. Drew eats one of them and shrinks down to the size of the little animals. She runs as fast as she can, out of the house and beyond.

Suddenly, Drew finds herself face-to-face with a puppy. She starts to play fetch with it, but she soon realizes that at her present size, the puppy poses a considerable threat. Drew barely manages to escape being trampled.

Drew finds a mushroom. One side of the mushroom will make her grow taller, and the other side will make her grow shorter. Drew is not sure which side is which, so she bites into one morsel. She is suddenly squashed down. She hastily eats the other morsel, and her body elongates tremendously.

Drew eats from each of the mushroom bits, using them to balance each other, until she brings herself to her normal size. She feels strange to be her correct size again, but she is pleased that she has made it to this point. She comes across a charming, miniature house. Drew wants to go inside, so she eats from the "short" mushroom bit until she is just nine inches tall. She enters the house but sees nothing which interest her so she leaves and begans to walk down the road.

Drew soon runs into a Cheshire cat, whom she asks for directions. After receiving some odd directions, Drew wanders in the woods until she finds a tree with a door in it. She goes inside and finds herself in the long hallway again. This time, she's prepared. She takes the key from the glass-topped table and unlocks the door to the garden. She then eats just enough mushroom so that she can step through the door, and she finds herself in a lovely garden. Drew's past experiences has taught her how to manipulate herself and her environment to fit her needs.

Drew enters the garden and finds three gardeners, shaped like playing cards, hurriedly painting the white roses of a rose tree. Drew asks why they are painting the roses red, and one of the gardeners admits to her that the tree was supposed to have been a red rose tree. If the queen learns about the error, she will cut off their heads.

The queen's procession arrives. When the queen sees the unpainted roses, she orders the guards to behead the gardeners. The soldiers come forward, and the gardeners run to Drew for protection. Drew secretly hides them in a large flowerpot but the soldiers find them and takes them away to court.

Drew finds herself in court as a defendant because of her efforts in trying to help the gardeners. The King of Hearts is the judge, and the jurors are various animals, some of whom Drew has already met. The White Rabbit recites the nursery rhyme about the Knave of Hearts helping to hide from the Queen of Hearts. This is the same accusation placed against the Drew.

Drew gets up. Forgetting how large she has grown, she knocks over the jury box by accident. She puts the box upright again, and puts all the jurors back into place. The king begins to cross-examine her, bombarding her with bad logic. Drew remains completely composed and is able to point out some of the inconsistencies in what he says.

Drew speaks up throughout the presentation of evidence. When the queen calls out for her beheading, Drew declares that she is not afraid; after all, they are only a pack of cards. Suddenly all the cards rise up and fly into her face.

Drew then wakes up. She has been dreaming. She tells her sister about all of her strange adventures in Wonderland and then runs into her house to have her tea.

This tale emphasizes the growth we must all go through. We all have or have had growing pains. We are all learning from our experiences. The learning may be painful or enjoyable, and at times, in one way or another, we resist the growing. In the story, Drew struggles to adapt to the rules of her new world, a world much older than herself. There are strange new rules and behaviors. She is clumsy, trying to live in this new world because she is unfamiliar with her surroundings and with what she should do. It is a world controlled by adults who sometimes do not have the best intentions toward children. The child's challenge is to learn the complex rules of this world.

And as we travel from childhood to adolescence, we must hang on. Our adolescence is a turbulent time. Adolescents are in search of themselves, trying to gain control and not knowing what they should do. Adolescents are on the verge of adulthood and not quite equipped to take on adult responsibilities but eager to have adult privileges. There are new challenges and new responsibilities.

As adolescents grow into adulthood, they learn to adapt physically, emotionally, intellectually, and, most important, morally. Moral maturity consists of empathy, conscience, a sense of community, and responsibility. As maturation progresses, adolescents learn what is just and unjust. In the tale, Drew's morality matures as demonstrated by how she is appalled by the injustice of the court proceedings. It is a mark of compassion in her growth as a person that she will refuse to be intimidated by those of status.

As you move toward adulthood, there is an abrupt, almost violent physical change coupled with the emotional chaos of trying to blend the worlds of adolescence and adulthood, two worlds that are not compatible. You may experience an identity crisis, one that comes with the inability to identify who you are supposed to be in relation to what others want you to be.

And just when you think you have it under control, the growing starts again. Many young people feel that if they were only adults, they could handle things better. They soon learn that each age has its own unique challenges, and that some of the things they accomplished when young, is the best. Along with growth comes wisdom. Intelligence can be learned but wisdom comes with age and experience. True wisdom is demonstrated by adaptability. Our identity changes and adjusts as we experience life.

Life doesn't come with labels and instructions on how to solve problems. People's emotions and thoughts are not labeled. You have to figure them out for yourself, usually through experience. There will not be magical solutions to ingest to make your problems disappear. There are no magical keys that will unlock doors to the passages of your journey forward.

8

Drew Barrymore: A Popular Princess

"Life is very interesting…in the end,
some of your greatest pains, become your greatest strengths."
—Drew Barrymore

Baby Girl

Drew Blythe Barrymore was born on February 22, 1975, in Los Angeles County, California. She is the daughter of actor John Drew Barrymore Jr. and Ildiko Jaid. Drew has two half-sisters, Jessica and Blythe Barrymore, and a half-brother, John Barrymore. Drew's great-grandparents were actors Maurice Barrymore and Georgiana Drew. Her grandparents were actors John Barrymore and Dolores Costello.

The director Steven Spielberg is her godfather. Drew's mother, Jaid, was also an actress and is known as the author of a book that she dedicated to Drew.

Drew was born into one of most famous acting and drinking families. Her family line consists of famous people in the film industry who drank their lives away. Her father, John Barrymore Jr., stopped his acting career because of alcoholism. He left his daughter, Drew, when she was an infant to pursue drugs and alcohol. Drew's great-great grandfather, John Drew, grandfather John Barrymore Sr., great-aunt Ethel, great-uncle Lionel Barrymore, and aunt Diana all died from alcohol-related issues.

Drew's father, John, had a history of getting into trouble dating back to before Drew was born. His marriage to Drew's mother, Jaid, was his second marriage. A week after John Barrymore married his first wife, actress Cara Williams, he was tossed into jail for a domestic dispute. He was arrested on several counts of drunk driving and hit and run. His unrestrained alcoholism cost him his good standing with Actor's Equity. In 1960 he had moved to Rome.

Upon returning to the United States, he met Jaid at the Troubadour nightclub in Los Angeles. Soon after, they began living together in West Hollywood and then married. Their time together was violent. Jaid thought that she would be able to rehabilitate him and reform the temper that drove him to drink and use drugs. She tried to get him into treatment and therapy. None of this helped. She became the target of his anger. The more she tried to love him, the more he lashed out at her. She eventually had his baby, Drew, thinking that a family and responsibility would motivate him to control his behavior.

Drew's mother found that this did not motivate John; instead, it enraged him. Jaid left John. Before she left, John made a promise to Jaid. He stated, "If you leave me, if you hurt me by leaving, I'm going to hurt you back by making sure that your child's life is miserable"(Barrymore, 38). Whether or not he consciously intended it, he cast a tragic shadow over his little girl. He was a puzzle Drew was not able to comprehend, a mystery she learned to accept as a painful part of her life.

Jaid, estranged from her husband, began taking her daughter to auditions when she was a baby. A friend of Drew's mother snapped a photo of Drew and showed it to a children's theatrical agent, who was impressed. This prompted an immediate response with a date and time for a job interview. At first Jaid was against Drew entering the business. She first rejected the idea but was then persuaded by her friend that this could be an opportunity for Drew. Drew was offered the first four commercials for which she auditioned.

Drew didn't waste much time getting in front of the cameras, making her first commercial when she was nine months old and her first television movie, *Suddenly Love*, at the age of two. Two years later, she made her film debut, appearing in *Altered States*. At the age of seven, Drew became a true celebrity in her role as Gertie in Steven Spielberg's *E. T. The Extra-Terrestrial*. The huge success of that 1982 film introduced Drew to millions of people. She then received leads in two more films, *Irreconcilable Differences* and *Firestarter*.

John and Jaid's relational difficulties caused Drew to have an unusual upbringing. She spent lots of time with her mother at different parties and seldom saw her father. This, in addition to the pressure of child stardom, contributed to Drew's developing numerous self-destructive habits.

When she was four years old, Drew expressed to her mother that she wanted to act. She loved being part of a group. Because of the abondment by her father and her mother being scarce during her developmental years, Drew loved the bond she made with fellow actors while working on a movie. Working on a movie was like being a part of a really large group or family.

Drew's need to be liked and to be accepted made her vulnerable in an egocentric way. Egocentric thinking causes a child to take everything personally and to have a vulnerable ego. The impact of not having her parents' time created a feeling of being worthless. She felt that she was worth less than their time, attention, or direction. Young children's egos are affected by how they perceive events. Drew saw her parent's lack of time as rejection. A child might think, if mom and dad are not with me, it's because of me. There must be something wrong with me, or they would want to be with me. They must be angry at me, and that is why they left.

One's ego becomes vulnerable when one has not developed ego boundaries. An ego boundary is an internal strength by which a person guards his or her inner space. Without boundaries, a person has no protection. Strong boundaries keep the person in control of who enters that person's world. A person with weak ego boundaries gives control over to others and to outside events. Strong boundaries result from identification with parents who themselves have strong boundaries. Parents with weak boundaries raise vulnerable, insecure children.

Children develop experiences as they grow. They use their parents' experiences as a guide. They depend on their parents to identify what they should and should not do, and how they should react to outside stimuli. As they internalize their parents' words and behaviors, children form a dependable guide inside themselves. If the parent is not dependable, the child will not develop this inner resource.

Children mirror their caretakers. Mirroring means that someone is there, reflecting back to us who we really are at any given moment. In the first three years of our life especially, we seek information about ourselves and our value. We build a foundation on which to develop who we are. This foundation needs to be strong; otherwise, everything that is built on it will be weak. Our parents become the mirror in which our reflections identify who we are. We see ourselves in what our parents reflect us to be. Our parents' reactions toward us help us to define our perceptions of ourselves. Drew's mirror was cracked and flawed, resulting in a negative, distorted self-image.

Because of the stress and fast pace of the entertainment industry, the young actress began to succumb to a destructive lifestyle defined by drugs, alcohol, and too much partying. Drew was a child expected to behave like an adult. She began drinking at the age of nine and started taking drugs a short while later.

Sucked In, Sucked Dry

As children, we look to have our love needs met within the family. If our parents behave in any way that threatens our well-being, if they express anger, impatience, contempt, indifference, or neglect, or if they abuse us in any way, we feel something is wrong with us. As children, we assume we are at fault, not them. Little by little, we come to experience the world in much the same way we view our parents.

Drew learned from her parents. Her mother threw herself into her work, and her father was an angry alcoholic. As children, we emotionally internalize our parents' behavior in order to be accepted by them and in order to ensure continued protection against abandonment or rejection. Children do not recognize or acknowledge the inadequacies and faults of their parents. They need to believe their parents are right in order to ensure security.

Unfortunately, a wide range of adverse factors in Drew's environment produced insecurity. Drew experienced erratic behavior on the part of her parents: lack of respect for her needs, lack of guidance, disparaging attitudes, too much admiration—or the absence of it, lack of reliable personal warmth, parental disagreements that forced her to take sides, too much and too little responsibility, lack of adequate protection, unkept promises, and a hostile atmosphere during the times her father was present.

Drew remembers an early experience of her father coming home. She and her mother were standing in the kitchen. Her father made a dramatic appearance. Although she had not seen him in a while, she called out to him. He was drunk and growled at her. He looked threatening to her. It was at this time that she began to learn what her father was really like (Barrymore, 37). Our early experiences with our parents have a profound effect on our lives, shaping our self-image, attitudes, moods, and behavior. We develop our survival strategies and life orientations as a result of these experiences. They condition us. Not only are we unable to recognize or acknowledge the faults or abusive behavior of our parents, we often imitate these faults and inadequacies (attitudes, moods, and behaviors) in order to be accepted by our parents.

More than merely role models, parents are everything to little children. As children, we identify emotionally with our parents. But parents are only human, with negative behavioral patterns as well as positive ones. Drew knew this only too well. Her interactions with her father were emotionally and physically abusive. Drew has reported that her mother hated talking about her father, no matter how much Drew pleaded. She learned about her father gradually, in bits and pieces, over the years. "I can actually remember seeing my father only a handful of times, the last time was when I was seven years old. I had a pretty good idea why it was dangerous to be around him." "In a blur of anger he roared into the room and threw my mother to the ground. Then he turned on me. He picked me up and threw me against the wall. Luckily half of my body landed on the big sack of laundry and I wasn't hurt. My daddy didn't even look back at me. He turned and grabbed a bottle of tequila, shattered a bunch of glasses all over the floor and stormed out of the house." Drew seldom saw him sober. But she kept hoping, loving her father and trying to get love in return (Barrymore, 30).

Among mammals, humans require the longest period of care and nurture from adults. In fact, we cannot survive our first several years without continuing physical and emotional parental care. Our very lives depend upon the care and nurture we receive from our parents, emotionally as well as physically. Children need to feel that they will not be abandoned and that they are loved and valued by their parents or parental figures.

Drew remembers that one time when she was with her father, he took her hand and stuck it in a candle flame. It burned and she started to cry. Her cries seem to make him even angrier (Barrymore, 52). Instead of giving her comfort, her father threatened her. He did not bring her warmth and security but rather danger and fear. She wanted love from him but never received it. When she didn't get that love, she assumed it was her fault. No one told her anything different.

Drew has a half-brother, John on her fathers side. Whenever she had seen him, he would ask for money. He behaved strangely and was wild like their father. He would play with her and then, out of nowhere, erupt into a temper tantrum, leaving Drew to wonder what she had done wrong (Barrymore, 49).

The only time Drew was able to experience normal family life was with other families, never with her own. One time, while on a shoot in North Carolina, Drew stayed with the Ward family. She convinced herself that she was part of the Ward family, which gave her a tremendous since of security and comfort. She liked having a dad, a brother, and a big family. It was what she imagined a family would be like, which made saying good-bye to them difficult at the end of the shoot.

Later, Drew received mental health treatment to address her emotional issues. The biggest issue Drew had to contend with in treatment was her interaction with her parents and the messages she had learned from them. We keep alive parental messages by judging ourselves based on those messages. We try to cover up our poor opinions of ourselves by being perfect. Drew was desperate for love and approval and would do anything to make people like her. Wanting others to like her, she remained loyal in situations and relationships even when it was evident that her loyalty was undeserved. An individual such as Drew can be intimidated by angry people and personal criticism. These behaviors caused her to feel inadequate and insecure. Denial, isolation, control, shame, and inappropriate guilt are legacies from Drew's family.

School Times

Drew had a lot of difficulty in school as an adolescent. Because of her acting, she changed schools often. She hated going to new schools. She would always be the new kid on the block, accompanied by whispers and stares. In addition, Drew had been exposed to more experiences than the average child. Being with other children was stifling. In contrast to the independence she experienced on the set, she was suddenly expected to settle down in school.

Once, in front of the entire class, a teacher told her that she would end up as a failure. "I wanted to crawl inside myself and die. But there was no escape. I vowed not to show any emotion, though. I sat there stone-faced, crying on the inside and completely humiliated" (Barrymore, 99).

If that wasn't enough to ruin whatever self-image she had, there was a nasty group of boys who constantly tortured her. They delighted in belittling her. Their torment was endless. Jealousy was the only reason for their behavior. Almost daily, they would hit her with books and call her names like "fatso" and "fat-ass pig." This hurt her deeply, but she did not have the self-confidence to strike back. When people said awful things to her, she took them as gospel. Instead of telling them to take a hike, she just took in the hurtful remarks, until eventually she let them completely undermine everything she knew to be true.

No matter how much she complained, she had to go to school. She was trapped between the boys who picked on her, the teacher who humiliated her, and her mother, who didn't understand why she was bringing home poor grades. She went to school disheveled and ashamed. Her grades did not reflect the ability of a person who had a photographic memory. Drew complained constantly about the group of boys who insisted on making her life miserable. Eventually the parents met with the school, but the problem was not resolved. Getting stoned became Drew's alternative to her psychological distress at school. Marijuana and alcohol made things easier.

When Drew was a senior, she went to a new school. Many of the students in this school smoked cigarettes and pot. They had cars and rejected anything that prevented them from having fun. Out of self-preservation, Drew looked for an environment that gave her the kind of support she needed. That meant going to clubs, and she went out regularly. Drew would drink from open bottles left around while at these clubs. Her mother wanted her to stay at home, but Drew would storm out anyway, leading to numerous arguments.

When hanging out with her friends, Drew would do anything to strengthen her status with them. If it meant shutting her mother out of her life, then that is what she would do. Drew found herself becoming increasingly alienated from her mother. It was inevitable. There was so much she had hidden from her mother that they were strangers. The whole process of shutting down her emotions and excluding her mother from her life was a slow, painful one. She wanted to get stoned everyday. When they clashed, her mother became the villain, the cause of all her unhappiness.

Negative Love

Drew harbored resentment and hostility toward her mother. Her mother had failed to find a replacement for her father. She had failed to find a mate who could provide Drew with the paternal affection she so desperately craved.

Drew never gave up on her father. She'd talk about him all of the time. Her mother became the object of her complaints and anger about their divorce. Drew begged her mother to reconcile with her father, but this was not a possibility. Drew decided that because he left her, she was the bad person. She didn't know the whole story behind the breakup, and her mother tried to spare her by not telling her. Drew became very resentful toward her mother.

When we as children experience a parent's love being cut off (e.g., through divorce, abandonment, death, imprisonment, or through their love becoming conditional), the parental bond is broken. We feel unlovable, as if a part of us has died. We take these experiences into our adulthood, feeling unlovable. When we have positive experiences as children, in which we bond in a healthy way with our parents, we also take these positive experiences into adulthood. As adults, our love relationships with others come from our experiences as children and from what we have learned from these experiences. Because of her father's behavior, the love Drew experienced with her father was negative love.

In our relationships, we unconsciously try to recapture our parents' love, choosing partners who manifest the same traits. We project our parents unconsciously and automatically onto our lovers, authority figures, bosses, friends, colleagues, or teachers. The result of this projection is resistance, conflict, giving and receiving rejection, heartbreak, loss, and most of all pain.

Many adults act like frightened children who would do almost anything to avoid pain. As adults, we do not have to withdraw or pretend the pain does not exist. Unfortunately, we often spend our lives avoiding the causes of problems in our lives, afraid that facing our pain will hurt too much and hoping that it will somehow just disappear.

Because of Drew's father's own childhood programming, he did not know how to nourish Drew. He had not received the affection and guidance he needed from his parents. He was never taught to honor, respect, and love himself, so how could he give to Drew what he never had? Had he been able to respect himself, maybe he would have been able to give Drew the nurturing she needed to build a strong sense of inner security.

Drinking and Drugging

Drew found security at nightclubs and parties, and in alcohol. Her addiction helped her medicate the pain she felt from the rejection and abuse she frequently experienced. As a teenager her substance use was out of control and had begun to affect every part of her life. She was no longer a cute, jubilant child, and no one seemed to notice or to care.

People who interact with teenagers in the home or community need to be alert to changes in a teenager's behavior and appearance that may signal substance use.

By recognizing the potential warning signs and symptoms of substance use, you may be able to get help for a teenager in need of treatment.

Drug use is associated with a variety of negative consequences, including increased risk of serious drug use later in life, school failure, and poor judgment, all of which put teens at risk for accidents, violence, unplanned and unsafe sex, and suicide.

Personality change, sudden mood changes, irritability, irresponsible behavior, low self-esteem, poor judgment, and a general lack of interest are associated with alcohol and drug use. Other symptoms include starting arguments or withdrawing from the family, decreased interest, negative attitude, and discipline problems. Substance users search for friends who are less interested in standard home and school activities.

Treatment is usually necessary at this point. Treatment should take into account family factors that increase the risk for substance abuse problems in youth, such as any history of parental or sibling substance abuse, including addiction, domestic violence, neglect, and physical, sexual, or emotional abuse. Drew's father had displayed many of the above precipitants that would predispose Drew to substance use.

The fact that Drew was in trouble was finally noticed, and she received help. Drew thought she was a well-adapted individual but found out that she was a vulnerable kid, bruised and tender on the inside, a kid who refused to acknowledge the tremendous pain that had built up inside her and had been ignored over time. In a bit of twisted logic, she had dealt with that reality by not dealing with it and by numbing herself with alcohol and drugs.

She started smoking cigarettes when she was nine. Soon afterward, she graduated to alcohol. She started drinking with friends when she slept at their homes. After a while, drinking was the only way she could have fun. She not only drank to have fun but to numb her pain.

At age nine, Drew had her first experience passing out from drinking. She was at a party for her third movie, *Firestarter*, when she downed two glasses of champagne. While filming *Babes in Toyland*, Drew spent her time off getting drunk in her hotel suite. She started smoking pot at age eleven. The next year, she tried cocaine.

A precipitant to Drew's alcohol and drug use was going to night clubs like Studio 54 and the China Club with her mother. This is where Drew developed a preteen fondness for drugs and alcohol. At around the same time, when her movie *Far from Home* finished shooting, she ran away, using her mother's credit card. She was thirteen and spiraling out of control.

When she was fourteen, after consuming fifteen beers Drew's mother sent her to an ASAP Family Treatment Center, a drug and alcohol rehabilitation facility in Van Nuys, California. Just twelve days later, she left treatment to finish filming another movie, *See You in the Morning*. Once that film was completed, she returned to the treatment center. After being sober for seventy-eight days, she relapsed by using cocaine, which resulted in her being handcuffed and taken back to the center where, this time, she stayed for three months. Once she left the center, she started getting high again. She slashed her wrists and was rushed to the hospital. She spent the next forty-five days in ASAP treatment. She would later write about her experiences in her book, *Little Girl Lost*.

The higher she got, the happier she imagined herself to be, and the more miserable she actually was. We all have negative moods, attitudes, and behaviors that emanate from a very deep emotional level. They often reflect our feeling of being unlovable. Every day, in all areas of our lives, we act out negative emotional needs, preconceptions, and attitudes based on childhood programming. The pain and conflict caused by these negative attitudes, feelings, and behaviors result in personal suffering.

Who Am I Really?

Drew began to wonder how she could ever like herself. In these moments, she began to realize how estranged she had become from herself, not to mention from the rest of the world. This sent her into a spiraling depression. Much of the depression came from feelings of shame. Shame and guilt are powerful. They produce feelings of embarrassment, blame, responsibility for negative circumstances, and regret about real or imagined misdeeds. Shame and guilt can lead an individual to have exaggerated personality traits in certain areas. A person can become overly responsible, striving to make life right. When this happens, you are willing to do anything to make everyone happy. You become obsessed with the tenuous nature of your personal actions, words, and decisions. You can become so overcome by the fear of doing, acting, saying, or being wrong that you eventually choose inactivity and silence. You become a poor decision maker. It is so important to always be right in your decisions that you become unable to make a decision because it may be a wrong one. Drew experienced most of the above.

Because she was left with a babysitter most of the time, Drew felt abandoned. Her mother had an acting career. When she quit her acting, she became Drew's manager. This further confused Drew. First she felt abandoned by her mother.

Now she was feeling that her worth to her mother was based on how much money she made.

"I'd ride along in cars with my friends and their mothers and wished my life would be like theirs. When I was dropped off I would run inside to my babysitter. Our house seemed so empty, quiet, and lonely. My mom was off working and my dad was out of his mind" (Barrymore, 12). The circumstances of her life fed her insecurities and contributed to her low self-esteem.

It took a while before she could admit to herself that her drive to succeed was based on a deep-seated need to feed her insecurities and low self-esteem. She needed constant affirmation that she had worth. In succeeding as an actress she felt wanted. She had a following of fans who not only wanted to see her act, they wanted to be her. She felt valued in knowing that she was talented enough to get acting jobs, and when she was working she was a part of an elite group in doing so.

It is unfortunate when individuals such as Drew feel their worth depends on achieving certain goals. Achieving a goal does not sustain self-esteem for long. A person who feels noble today because of having obtained some goal or success will feel equally inadequate and self-despising tomorrow when a slight failure occurs. Drew's self-perceived "value" as a person was determined by satisfying some external goal. And when she failed to reach an external goal, as eventually happened, her life seemed worthless.

People who define their value based on their successful acts develop faulty thinking. Drew felt that her self-esteem could be earned. This is not an uncommon perception. Not only do most individuals believe that self-esteem must be earned, but also that it must be reinforced repeatedly and tirelessly if it is to survive within their psychological framework.

Regardless of how magnificent our performance is at any specific endeavor, our feelings of increased self-worth following such an accomplishment are almost invariably short-lived. No feat of bravery, act of heroism, or display of superior talent will bless the individual with permanent self-esteem. This was a lesson Drew learned.

A majority of people believe that if they could gloriously achieve this or that in their lifetime, such an accomplishment would forever rid them of intermittent feelings of inadequacy. Whatever the objective, it is foolish to believe that any achievement will provide more than a temporary, fleeting sensation of positive self-esteem.

When people base their self-esteem on specific behaviors or accomplishments, they must constantly strive for, and perpetually achieve, new goals if their ego intoxication is to continue. A person is then constantly in need of reassurance. Drew's work provided her with this reassurance.

The public saw Drew Barrymore as a movie star; she viewed herself quite differently. She saw herself as a sad, lonely, and unattractive girl. She was good at hiding her insecurities. Feelings of insecurity can turn us into someone we really are not and make us less than what we should be.

People hide their insecurities in many ways. Drew dealt with her insecurities by becoming the life of the party. Being an extrovert was her way of keeping an inner hurt from being discovered. She felt that if people didn't see the real her, they couldn't hurt the real her. Her insecurity fed upon itself.

The more insecure you feel, the more pathetic you'll appear to be. The more pathetic you seem, the more insecure you'll feel, and so on. Drew felt a lot of pain associated with living with insecurity. Her insecurity caused her to have the following emotions, all of which are common with people who are insecure:

- A sense of helplessness in the face of problems, conflict, or concerns

- A belief that you are inadequate or incompetent to handle life's challenges

- A fear of being discovered as inadequate, ill-fitted, or unsuited to meet responsibilities at home, school, or on the job

- A sense of not fitting in with your peer group

- A perception that life is unpredictable

- A sense of lacking support or reinforcement where you live, work, or play

Drew's upbringing was unstable, causing her to have abnormal experiences that produced numerous insecurities. She was raised in a chaotic, unpredictable, and volatile environment, where she was kept off balance, on guard, or on edge. She experienced a major loss of her father's affection and had a difficult time in accepting this loss and adjusting to it. People had an unrealistic list of rules and expectations for her, making her feel successful for only short periods of time. She developed a poor body image, which made her believe that others saw her in a negative light. This made her feel self-conscious, tense, and anxious in dealing with others.

She was given very little direction, guidance, or discipline in her earlier years, leaving her unable to cope with the pressures of life. Being raised in such unhealthy conditions may result in difficulties in establishing healthy, long-lasting relationships. You become a victim of fears that impair the freedom of action or choice.

Drew grew up an only child, raised by a single, working parent. She was always insecure, feeling that people didn't like her. How could they when her father hated her? As she got older, the problems became magnified, making it harder for her to deal with them. Her feelings of insecurity grew between film projects when there was no work. Without the ego boost of work, she used liquor and drugs to try to run from everything or to numb it. She was the party girl on the run. When she was high everything was fine.

Putting Away the Toys

Drew became accustomed to the nightlife of Los Angeles. Party invitations were plentiful. She had to go to various publicity events and openings. The party-time environment was intoxicating. She loved it. As the partying increased, the acting job offers decreased.

Observers began writing Drew off as just another failed child star when she was barely into her teens. She made a string of mediocre movies, many of which only reinforced her image as a has-been.

While in the same rehabilitation clinic she attended previously, Drew wrote an autobiography, *Little Girl Lost*, which detailed her experiences with drugs and alcohol as she was growing up. Her goals were simple: to stay sober and live a good life. Her book went all the way to number one on the best-seller list. Her drug and alcohol problems came to a halt, and she became legally emancipated from parental control. While not working on movies, she worked in a coffee-house and in a music store. In the early 1990s, she entered another phase in her career, gaining notoriety for playing a series of lowly Lolitas. Although the characters were not flattering, she turned in good performances in the movies *Motorama*, *Doppelganger: The Evil Within*, *Sketch Artist*, *Guncrazy*, *Poison Ivy*, *No Place to Hide*, *Wayne's World*, and *Batman Forever*, all of which featured her in seductive roles. In 1993, she did an ad campaign for Guess Jeans.

Drew was transforming from an insecure teen to a self confident adult. Her on-screen talents were complemented by the off-screen reputation she was building for herself as a daredevil who never held back. First, she could be seen posing nude with then-boyfriend Jamie Walters on the cover of *Interview Magazine*, then modeling for a series of Calvin Klein ads. She then flashed David Letterman during an appearance on *The Late Show* as a "birthday present" to the host. Finally, she posed nude for *Playboy* in 1995. Drew wanted to be perceived as a woman who knew what she wanted. The following year, she started her own production company, Flower Films Inc., with her partner, Nancy Junoven, and acted in the movie *Bad Girls*.

Drew began to communicate openly with her mother. She felt a sense of liberation from getting everything out in to the open. Feeling that a lot of families are not able to be open and honest about damages, guilt, and other secrets, she felt that it was necessary to expose her feelings and purge herself. If families are able to acknowledge some of the dysfunctions, it can open up family members and bring them closer together.Drew knew how it was to hide her feelings and have secrets. "Life was like a vicious confrontation and evasions. I'd put on this nauseatingly sweet act whenever I was around my mom. It was all a fake.I didn't want her to know how much pain and trouble I was in(Barrymore 18).

Her cinematic luck began to change in 1995 when she turned in a solid performance in *Boys on the Side* with Whoopi Goldberg and Mary-Louise Parker. In the same year, she made a memorable, terror-filled appearance in the blockbuster *Scream* and costarred in Woody Allen's musical, *Everybody Says I Love You*. In 1998, she costarred in the popular comedy *The Wedding Singer*, with Adam Sandler, and in *Ever After*, a version of the Cinderella story, costarring Anjelica Huston as her evil stepmother.

Her career began its recovery with roles such as those in *Poison Ivy*, *2000 Malibu Road*, and *The Amy Fisher Story*. Drew Barrymore has continued to persevere through adversity. Her persistence and energy have helped her recover from the difficulties of growing up in front of the camera and the public eye and have shaped her into a strong woman.

A Hop and a Skip

In 1995, Barrymore's image underwent an abrupt and effective transformation from slut to sweetheart. With a brief but memorable role in Wes Craven's *Scream* and a lead in Woody Allen's *Everyone Says I Love You* that featured her as a Kelly Girl for the 1990s, Barrymore's career received an adrenaline shot to the heart. She began working steadily again, and she reshaped her off-screen persona into that of a delightful and sweet-natured girl trying to mend her ways. This new image was supported by her screen work, much of which featured her as a chaste heroine. Her starring role as Cinderella in *Ever After* (1998) was a hit. Barrymore's other major 1998 film, *The Wedding Singer*, was another hit, further enhancing her reputation as America's new sweetheart. The following year, the actress put to rest her wild child reputation. She solidified her reputation as America's sweetheart when she starred as the nerdy, lovelorn, twenty-something reporter in *Never Been Kissed*, the first movie she had produced. Her newfound self-esteem has brought her back from her past problems when she was a young teenager.

Drew's next movie from Flower Films was *Charlie's Angels*. Although some may have thought her transition from sweetheart to skull-cracker in *Charlie's Angels* might have signaled a shift toward more action-oriented roles, Barrymore once again charmed audiences with another emotional comedy, *Riding in Cars with Boys* (2001). Drew voiced for *Titan A. E.* (2000), a science-fiction adventure cartoon about the journey to find the human race. She also voiced for *Akima*, this time alongside Matt Damon. Her most recent films include *Date School*, *Fever Pitch*, and *Lucky You*.

In the summer of 2000, Barrymore, then twenty-five, became engaged to the eccentric, twenty-eight-year-old Canadian comic, Tom Green, of MTV's *The Tom Green Show*. Drew had stuck by Tom during his fight against cancer. After six months of marriage to Green, Green filed for divorce citing irreconcilable differences in December 2001. Drew Barrymore has proven to be a strong survivor, and so she continued on.

Mom Never Taught Me This

Drew's lessons started early, far before the age any child should have to learn such lessons. When others her age were playing games and flirting with boys, she was earning a living and socializing at an adult level, having skipped the usual developmental experiences.

But she did learn. She learned not only adult lessons but also those developmental lessons she had skipped. She backtracked to lay a foundation strong enough to build a healthier life than the one she once had. Sometimes the use of alcohol and drugs blurred these lessons, but the messages came through anyway, loud and clear. Drew learned from her mistakes. These are some of the lessons she learned:

"It's only through listening that you learn, and I never want to stop learning."

"I believe that everything happens for a reason, but I think it's important to seek out that reason—that's how we learn."

"I don't know anybody's road that's been paved perfectly for them, there are no manuals, you don't know what life has in store for you."

"My whole life, I've wanted to feel comfortable in my skin. It's the most liberating thing in the world."

"If you're going to be alive and on this planet, you have to, like, suck the marrow out of every day and get the most out of it."

"And when things come clear to you, no matter how you had to get there, as long as you come out the other side of it, then it's all worth it."

We've got to learn hard things in our lifetime, but it's love that gives you the strength. It's being nice to people and having a lot of fun and laughing harder than anything, hopefully every single day of your life.

"You've just got to do the best that you can."

"I have no regrets. Everything you've been through makes you what you are."

"If you're going to go through hell…I suggest you come back learning something."

It's My Life and I'll Play if I Want To

From the time Drew could walk and talk, she pursued a goal of being an entertainer. She had a seemingly natural talent. She refined her talents to become one of the most celebrated child-to-adult actresses of modern times. During her struggles, Drew pursued her dreams and became an accomplished actress and producer. Her life wasn't easy, in or out of the entertainment industry, but she persevered.

9

Waking Up with Sleeping Beauty

Once upon a time long ago there lived a king and queen in a beautiful palace with wide halls and high towers. All round the palace, for miles and miles, there were lovely gardens with terraces.

There was everything there that the heart could wish for, except a child. And this made the king and queen very sad. But at last, after many years, they had their wish, and a little baby daughter, Halle, was born, a beautiful child with a face like a rosebud and eyes that sparkled.

They immediately wanted to christen their baby and wanted fairies to be godmothers to the baby princess.

All had gathered for the christening. When they were just about to begin, there was a clashing of brazen claws and a rushing of wings. Something like a black cloud seemed to pass before the tall windows and darken all the room. Then the great doors burst open with a terrible bang, and an old fairy in a long, trailing black gown, with her face almost hidden in a black hood, jumped out of a black chariot drawn by fierce griffins and stalked up to the table.

The king turned pale, and the queen nearly fainted, for this was the spiteful fairy Tormentilla, who lived all alone. The poor queen had forgotten all about her and had never sent her an invitation.

They all tried to make the best of it. Another chair was brought for Tormentilla. Both the king and queen told her over and over again how very, very sorry they were not to have invited her to the christening.

Then they all went into the great tapestried room where the princess lay sleeping in her cradle, and the seven good fairies began to say what they each would give her.

The first stepped forward and said, "She shall always be as good as gold"; the second said, "She shall be the cleverest princess in the world"; the third added, "She shall be the most beautiful"; the fourth said, "She shall be the happiest"; the fifth followed, saying, "She shall have the sweetest voice that was ever heard"; the sixth added, "Everyone shall love her." Just then the wicked, old, cross Tormentilla strode over to the cradle with long quick steps and, shaking her black crooked stick at the king and queen said. "And I say that she shall prick her hand with a spindle and die of the wound!"

At this the queen fell on her knees and begged and prayed Tormentilla to call back her cruel words. Suddenly the seventh fairy, the youngest of all, who had hidden herself behind the curtains for fear that such a thing might happen, came out and said, "Do not cry, dear Queen; I cannot quite undo my cousin's wicked enchantment, but I can promise you that your daughter shall not die. She will fall asleep for a hundred years. And, when these are past and gone, a prince shall come and awaken her with a kiss."

So the king and queen dried their tears and thanked the kind fairy for her goodness, and all the fairies went back to their homes. Things went on much as usual in the palace. The queen was protective of Halle, and the king made a law that every spindle in the country should be destroyed, and that no more should be made. Anyone who had a spindle would be heavily punished, if not executed at once.

The years went by happily enough, until Princess Halle was almost eighteen years old. All that the six fairies had promised had come true, for she was the best and the prettiest and the cleverest princess in the world, and everybody loved her. And, indeed, by this time Tormentilla's spiteful words were almost forgotten.

Now, the king and queen had to go away for a few days. The princess became bored and started exploring the castle. At last she found herself at the top of a narrow winding stairway in a tall turret that seemed older than the rest of the palace. There sat a little old woman, wearing a high white cap and spinning at a wheel.

For some time the princess stood at the door, watching the old woman curiously. She could not imagine what the woman was doing, for the princess had never seen a spinning wheel before, since, the King had ordered them all destroyed.

Now, it happened that the poor old woman who lived in this tower had never heard the king's command, for she was so deaf that if you had shouted until you were hoarse she would not have been able to understand you. Then the princess pointed to the spindle and made the old woman understand that she wanted to try to see if she could make it work.

So the old woman nodded and got up from her seat, and the princess sat down and took the spindle in her hand. But no sooner had she touched the spindle than she pricked the palm of her hand with the point and sank down in a swoon. Immediately a deep silence fell around and the whole kingdom fell asleep.

Although the sun had been shining brightly when the princess took the spindle in her hand, no sooner had she pricked herself with the point than deep shadows darkened the sunny rooms and gardens. It was just as though night had overtaken them, but there was no one awake in or near the palace to heed whether it was dark or light.

And so the years went on, and on, and on, until a hundred years had passed, and the palace and its story were all but forgotten.

One morning, a king's son from a neighboring country came hunting with his men and horses. He found himself in a part of the country where he had never been before. In vain, he tried to retrace his steps. He only seemed to wander farther away in the wrong direction.

He came to a woodcutter's cottage and dismounted to ask his way. An old man who lived in this hut directed the prince toward the best way back. The young prince pointed to the thick woods ahead, and asked what lay beyond it. The old man told him that there was a legend that beyond the woods was an enchanted palace where a beautiful princess had lain sleeping for a hundred years, and whom a prince was to awaken with a kiss.

Curious, the prince went into the woods and found his way to the castle. There everyone was sleeping, the sentinels and soldiers in the courtyard, the cooks in the kitchen, and the pages and lords-and ladies-in-waiting in the corridors and chambers; and, in the great throne room, the king and queen lay sleeping.

The prince passed on, wondering more and more, till he came at length to the narrow staircase that led to the little tower in which Princess Halle had fallen asleep. He went inside and came to the greatest wonder of all, the beautiful sleeping lady in her glistening white robes. She was so beautiful that to see her almost took his breath away. Falling on his knees, he bent to kiss her cheek. And as he kissed her, she opened her lovely eyes and said, smiling, "Oh Prince! Have you come at last? I have had such pleasant dreams."

Then she sat up laughing and rubbing her eyes, and gave him her hand. They went hand in hand together down the stairs and along the corridors, till they came to the throne room. There the king and queen were rubbing their eyes. They kissed their daughter and welcomed the prince most gladly.

The whole palace woke. Everything went on exactly as though the spell had lasted a hundred seconds instead of one hundred years. The prince and princess were married amid great rejoicing, and lived happily ever after.

Much as the king and queen in the tale above, we tiptoe through life, even during the wonderful times, afraid that something will go wrong. When things are going right, we have the tendency to feel that something bad is about to happen. And sometimes we are right. But most of the time things are just fine—even perfect. We take away from good experiences by waiting for the bad to come, because this is what has happened in the past. When things seem right, our experience is that someone always comes along and messes it up, or something goes wrong. So we go on believing that good things never last, which makes us constantly anxious when we do have good times.

When we finally get what we want, after having prayed and worked for it for years, the value of what we have gained is so high that we tend to worry about losing it instead of enjoying the fact that we have it.

We have a tendency to focus on the negative instead of the positive. We should use the positives in our life to defeat any negatives that may exist. The positives in our life give us the tools and talents to overcome the obstacles we may experience. But, instead, we focus on the problem instead of the solution. It's important to make the best of any situation by focusing on the options and the solutions to a problem.

If you have identified someone as dangerous, you need to let that person go, even if he or she is a loved one. Do not humor people like this because you are afraid of them. Get rid of them altogether if possible. They will only cause you grief in the end. You have to let go of harmful people, even if you fear them. The tendency to treat the bad as good for fear of insulting them is a mistake.

The king and queen thought they could avoid their problem. You can't avoid the bad by running away from it. You have to face it head-on and resolve the situation; otherwise, it will eventually catch up with you. Pretending that it doesn't exist and suppressing it will not work either. It is just another way of resigning yourself to the threat of others and becoming their willing victim.

Unresolved situations always catch up with you and take you by surprise, especially if the problem is you. You may want to seek the advice of an objective outsider. Ask friends and family who are not involved in the situation and give their resposes serious thought. It is hard to look at a problem objectively if the problem is you or you are in the middle of it. Step away and ask for advice. You aren't asking to be rescued—you want to get an objective perspective, and you want to face whatever situation it is that is causing you trouble.

10

Halle Berry: Royal Beauty

"You gain and learn from every decision that you make."
—Halle Berry

Disqualified and Misunderstood

Halle Berry was born on August 14, 1966, in Cleveland, Ohio. Her father was African American and her mother Caucasian. Her mixed heritage would have a strong impact on her life. Her father, Jerome Berry, was a former hospital attendant and her mother, Judith Berry, was a psychiatric nurse. Halle has an older sister named Heidi. When researching her role as Dorothy Dandridge, Halle discovered that she and Dandridge were both born in the same Cleveland, Ohio, hospital. This was significant to her because she saw Dandridge as a role model.

Halle's mother and father were married in a time when interracial marriages were not popular, but they dealt with society's disapproval. The biggest problem would not be society, but rather Jerome's problem with alcohol. Jerome was regularly coming home intoxicated.

The couple argued constantly until they divorced when Halle was four years old. Her father deserted the family, and Halle and her sister were raised by their mother. Jerome returned to his family after being gone for four years, but nothing had changed. He behaved violently toward his wife and daughters, and he left them once again soon after his arrival. Throughout her adult life, Halle would have no contact with him. They were still estranged when he died in 2003.

Halle was a quiet, unassuming girl who loved to read. She didn't like bringing attention to herself. Her friends found her pleasant and easy to get along with. She wasn't a party girl, even though everyone wanted to go out with her. She preferred to stay at home. When Halle was in the fifth grade, her teacher, who was also African American, helped her to see the proud achievements of other black people. Halle learned a lot about black pride from this teacher.

Halle and her older sister, Heidi, spent the first few years of their childhood living in an inner-city neighborhood. Judith then moved her family to a predominantly white suburb of Cleveland. Halle's fair complexion had made her stand out in her previous neighborhood, but not as much as it did when her mother moved them out of the inner city into a white suburb.

Now, a little older and in a more conservative environment, Halle's difference was noticed. It was important to Halle that she was black and that others saw her as black. She did not want to be labeled as a mulatto, stuck in the middle and not quite belonging anywhere. Because the neighborhood she moved into was predominantly white, Halle and her sister were treated cruelly because of their dark skin. Halle made a point to make friends and to fit in. She was determined not to let the color of her skin get the better of her.

Halle was subjected to discrimination at her new school. Her early experiences with racism greatly influenced her desire to excel. She remembers an altercation when she was asked if she knew her mother was white. This disturbed her. Her peers also gave Halle names such as oreo and zebra. One day, her mother told her to look in the mirror. He mother taught her to be a proud black woman. Her mother taught her daughters not to accept labels that were derogatory in their meaning. Halle's mother felt that no one was better than her children. "Identify yourself as black because that is what people see," she told her children (Kenyatta, 2003).

Throughout high school, the determined Halle participated in a wide array of extracurricular activities, holding positions as newspaper editor, class president, and head cheerleader. This gave her the popularity and acceptance she needed. One year, she was chosen prom queen but was accused of stuffing the ballot box. The contest made her mixed race an issue and was resolved by what was an unfair solution: Halle was forced to share the title with a white student. Her school was not going to give the title to a black student, but school officials were willing to let her share it. Despite this humiliating and unfair attack, Halle began competing in formal beauty contests, winning many. Her first win was as Miss Teen All-American. She went on to win the coveted title of Miss Ohio. Luckily those running the state pageant did not have the same prejudicial attitude Halle had experienced in high school.

Halle had to share her high school contest, but she was officially the most beautiful woman in the state. As Miss Ohio, Halle won the chance to compete in the 1986 Miss USA pageant. She dazzled the judges with her poise, her stunning evening gown, and her swimsuit. It came as no surprise that she made it all the way to the finals. She was chosen as first runner-up in the Miss USA pageant. The Miss USA pageant was important because, unlike the other pageants, the winner of the Miss USA pageant went on to compete for the title of Miss Universe and the first runner-up competed for the title of Miss World. Halle didn't win the Miss World title, but she did walk away from that pageant with enough money to put herself through community college. She gained a lot of valuable experience in front of the camera and in the high-pressure situations a pageant produces. Halle would use this experience to embark on an acting career that would eventually make her one of the most famous former titleholders of all time.

All her life, Halle Berry has been valued for her beauty. She was an adorable child who grew up to be a beauty contest winner and later Revlon's spokeswoman. But Halle Berry's greatest achievement has been proving, time and time again, that she has the talent and the brains to be more than just a beautiful face.

When she was growing up, Halle had a positive perception of her physical attributes but finding her social identity was more complicated. Social identification is a process by which individuals classify themselves and others into different social categories. This classification process serves the function of segmenting and ordering the social environment, enabling individuals to locate or define themselves in that social environment. Halle was from two cultures, not quite fitting in either one.

Beauty and the Beast

Halle would eventually be very successful in her career, but her personal life would consist of one challenge after another, especially in the area of relationships. For a short time, Halle was involved in a stormy relationship with *Jungle Fever* costar Wesley Snipes before she married Atlanta Braves' outfielder David Justice in 1993. The couple met in 1992 when Justice requested her autograph. She gave him her phone number instead. Six months later, she proposed, and they were married on New Year's Day 1993.

It happened fast. Halle proposed to Justice a few months after they met, stating that asking David to marry her was a sign she was taking control of her life and relationships. She wanted to be the chooser and not the chosen. She stated it felt good with him right from the start. Before David, Halle had been in a hurtful relationship and was looking for solace and comfort. Halle felt she was in a continuous beauty contest, where men picked her the way pageant judges had. She was tired of being chosen by the wrong men for the wrong reasons.

Sadly their marriage faltered and ended bitterly in less than three years. The story behind their breakup was tragic, and it left Halle very vulnerable. Justice felt that Halle carried a lot of baggage from her previous relationships. He remarked that she was always suspicious and frequently threw tantrums. Halle stated the separation with David was painful; she had tried as hard as she could to make it work, but she could not control both her actions and his (Kenyatta, 2003).

Reporting that she feared for her personal safety and well-being, Halle asked a Santa Monica judge to protect her from David. She filed for a restraining order, alleging that the Atlanta Braves slugger had come to her Los Angeles home and had harassed her (eonline,2004). It was believed that she had experienced emotional abuse in her relationship with Justice and feared him even after their breakup. Their separation had been less than amicable, and Halle was apparently afraid that Justice might act violently. She feared for her personal safety and well-being. The restraining order forced Justice to stay 500 yards away from the actress. Justice moved into their Atlanta home, and Halle stayed in Los Angeles.

Halle filed for a divorce in 1997. Halle then became secretly engaged to Eric Benét, a jazz musician, in August 1999. The couple married in February 2001 and announced their separation two years later. Halle officially filed for divorce from Eric in April 2004. Although Halle has been lucky in her career, she has not been as lucky in her relationships. She has loved deeply, but love has not seemed to be enough. Was this love she was experiencing, or was it something else?

Love is not critical, abusive, controlling, manipulative, or demeaning. It is not an addiction. It does not involve taking a hostage or being taken hostage. Love is not being a doormat. And, most important, love is not disguised as emotional abuse. This was a lesson Halle needed to learn.

She needed to learn how to protect herself. It is vital for women to learn how to protect themselves and to start realizing that emotional abuse is not acceptable. All people deserve to be treated with respect and dignity. In order to do that, they need to start learning how to treat themselves in a kinder, gentler way. They need to start learning how to love themselves.

Many times abuse disguised as love is in the form of emotional abuse. Many women find that emotional abuse is difficult to describe or even talk about. People don't take it seriously because it cannot be seen, like bruises or broken bones. In this way, it is not looked at as being harmful. How can it be when no one can see it or touch it?

Emotionally abused women state that one of the biggest problems they face is that others seldom take their accounts of abuse seriously. Victims are most often told by the abuser that the treatment is for their own good. Abuse is not good for anyone.

Emotional abuse is the source of all other types of abuse. The most damaging aspect of physical, sexual, and mental abuse is the trauma to one's heart and soul from being betrayed by the people one loves and trusts. The most destructive form of emotional abuse is the emotional abuse we have learned to inflict upon ourselves. We learn to do this from past experiences. When we accept such behavior from others, we then treat ourselves the same way.

Emotions are a vital part of our being. We cannot be whole and healthy without having an emotionally honest relationship with ourselves. We don't know who we truly are if our relationships with our own emotions are twisted, distorted, and repressed.

Emotional abuse can be verbal or nonverbal. Verbal or nonverbal abuse of a spouse or intimate partner consists of more subtle actions or behaviors than does physical abuse. While physical abuse might appear to be worse, the scars of verbal and emotional abuse are internal, making it difficult to treat. Emotional abuse can be much more damaging than physical abuse.

Emotional abuse of a spouse or intimate partner may include:

- Threatening or intimidating to gain compliance
- Destruction of the victim's personal property and possessions

- Violence to an object or a pet, in the presence of the intended victim, as a way of instilling fear of further violence
- Yelling or screaming
- Name-calling
- Constant harassment
- Embarrassing, making fun of, or mocking the victim
- Criticizing or diminishing the victim's accomplishments or goals
- Telling the victim that he or she is worthless alone, without the abuser
- Excessive possessiveness
- Isolation from friends and family
- Excessive checking up on the victim to make sure he or she is at home or where the victim said he or she would be
- Saying hurtful things while under the influence of drugs or alcohol, and using the substance as an excuse to say the hurtful things
- Blaming the victim for how the abuser acts or feels
- Making the victim feel or believe there is no way out of the relationship

Most of us would like to think that effortless relationships exist. Whether it's a fantasy we have seen on television, our view of the friendships of others that appear to last forever, or our experience with parent/child bonds that supersede the need to understand one another, we would like to believe that our most intimate relationships are unconditional. We would like to think that our relationships are strong enough to withstand anything. But the truth is that, at some point in our lives, most of us need to face the fact that relationships require effort to keep them strong and positive, and that even wonderful, strong relationships can be destroyed.

Whether you're looking to improve a love relationship, familial connection, friendship, or work relationship, understanding your own personality and the personality of the other person involved in the relationship will bring a new dynamic to the situation. This will allow better understanding and communication. Although the different types of relationships have very different characteristics and specific needs, both parties in any relationship need to know who they are and who they are in the relationship with.

Halle stated that her relationships were bad. The men she dated didn't really care about her. She did what she wanted to do, and they pretty much ignored her. When she got married, she had to consider how her husband would react to her behavior and how it would affect him and their relationship. Halle attempted to know her husband and consider his needs. This was good, but the problem was that she did not consider her own needs, leaving her open to one abusive situation after another.

Relationships that did not seem bad at the time would later prove to be abusive for her. For example, she had an ex-boyfriend in Chicago who later sued her to recoup money he had given her. He stated it was a loan, but she stated it was a gift. In the end, the judge ruled in her favor because he did not have records to support his claim.

This man had been a very supportive boyfriend. He was a doctor and had been very generous to Halle, both financially and emotionally. She could count on him in the past, but now that she had made it on her own, he was turning against her. She had another boyfriend who tried to sell inaccurate personal information about her. She was very disappointed by the claims made by both men.

Halle's past not only included emotional abuse but physical abuse as well. A previous lover once hit her so hard she temporarily lost eighty percent of her hearing in her left ear. She still cannot hear as well out of her left ear. This is a reminder to her of how dangerous some relationships can be.

Relationships are the most fundamental part of human existence. Relationships make us both vulnerable and secure. This dynamic remains throughout our life, whether we are in a friendship, a romance, a marriage, or a relationship with our children or other extended family members.

Halle suffered a lot of pain from her relationships, which damaged her self-esteem. This caused her to contemplate committing suicide. She relates her pain to that of Dorothy Dandridge. Halle believes that Dandridge committed suicide because of experiencing the pain that can drive a person to give up altogether. "I know how a person can feel, so alone that she just wants to go to sleep, because I have been there," Halle has said, referring to the time, shortly after her divorce from David Justice, when she considered taking her own life (Ebony, 1999). She did not go through with it. She attributes her strength during those moments of weakness to her spiritual convictions, and to that fact that she realized she has a greater contribution to make. She feels that she will never visit that sad place again, and this is a pact she has made with God.

Halle wanted the basics in her relationships and marriage: someone who valued the institution of marriage and all that it means, who could be comfortable with her and who could share quiet moments with her. Her relationship with men, though, did not give her those quiet moments of peace and security. Although she saw a therapist after her divorce from David, for Halle, the real healing didn't begin until she learned to live with herself, by herself. It was a process of deep, often painful, self-evaluation. She had to face all the demons she'd been trying to push away all her life. She finally realized she couldn't run from them anymore. The time had come for her to face her demons and slay them or be slain by them.

When Halle found the courage to examine her life, however, what she discovered was very important. She realized that she had to stop blaming her father for all the things that were wrong in her relationships. While his absence was part of it, a lot had to do with her and her choices.

She hid her real feelings when talking about her relationships, from herself as well as from others. She felt there was a deeply spiritual being inside, but she was afraid to let that part of her be seen for fear of rejection and judgment and for fear of not being the person the public had made her out to be. She always presented herself as a person who was in a happy relationship. After all, she felt her relationships and her ability to please men was a measure of her self-worth. This was a miserable existence, however, since she always had to pretend.

She was terrified of leaving her twenties single and alone. She had a lot of anxiety about turning thirty and not being with someone. At that time, she was in the middle of a divorce and felt like a failure. She wanted a family desperately, but she thought her diabetes would prevent her from building the family she wanted. Halle's need to be a mother became stronger when she and Eric Benét became engaged. She became very maternal and wanted a child.

Halle seemed to need someone in her life to help identify who she was. She needed to be needed or else she felt like nothing. She was still using men to identify who she was, and when that was gone, her identity was destroyed. This put her into a pattern of being codependent. Codependence is characterized by dependence on outer or external sources for self-worth and self-definition. This external dependence, combined with unhealed childhood emotional wounds, is activated whenever an emotional button is pushed, causing a person to be codependent and to live life in reaction to others. When people who are codependent behave in this way, they give others power over them.

Codependency leaves one vulnerable to emotional abuse, which can occur as a consistent pattern of unfair and unjust treatment or as a one-time traumatic event that remains unresolved. When an individual is degraded and controlled, he or she is being abused. Whether the abuser is behaving consciously or unconsciously, all abuse is about control, and emotional abuse is no exception.

Look how emotional abuse affected Halle. We might not have seen Halle Berry at the Academy Awards a few years ago if she had stayed in her garage just a little longer. The Oscar and Golden Globe winner says she was so depressed after her bitter divorce from David Justice that she came very close to killing herself. "The thought of my mother when I was in that moment in—sitting in the car. I was going to asphyxiate myself in a garage. When I was sitting there, really—with all my heart, wanting to end my life, I thought of my mother and I thought, Wow. How unfair. I would break her heart. My heart's broken and I'm going to kill myself. I would break her heart (King, 2002). Halle believes she became suicidal because she was still using men to identify who she was. When they were gone, she was nothing.

It is important to note the timing of her suicidal thoughts. Her desire to die occurred when she had just won a Golden Globe award and had been nominated for an Oscar. This is an actor's dream, the ultimate goal and accomplishment for someone in her profession. Yet, because she was not successful in her romantic relationship, she felt there was nothing to live for. What she had accomplished was irrelevant. All of her hopes lay externally in someone else—a man.

Human beings establish relationships with others for support, comfort, companionship, and a sense of belonging. When abuse is present, these needs are not met and damage occurs. Emotional abuse can occur in almost any relationship, but it is especially common in those where a power difference exists. The power differential does not have to be real, only imagined. It is most often perpetrated by spouses, intimate partners, parents, siblings, friends, teachers, employers, and, in spiritual communities, by the clergy and others in positions of influence.

Abuse from those we love is very damaging. One of the most significant results of abuse is low self-esteem. The abused person begins to feel helpless and hopeless. People with low self-esteem will habitually give in to the wishes of others because they distrust their own ability to make decisions. This makes them more likely to depend on the abuser. A person with high self-esteem is not easily controlled by someone else.

Another result of abuse is lack of self-confidence. People with low self-confidence are unable to make decisions on their own. They will seek out others to validate their judgment, and they will give in to someone else's persuasive arguments, even though it goes against their gut feeling. It is self-confidence that allows a person to experience risk and recover from failure, because the self-confident person believes in his or her own ability to learn and succeed.

For somewhat similar reasons, a victim of abuse can succumb to a failure syndrome or to a self-fulfilling prophecy. A failure syndrome exists when a person who does not feel good enough to succeed subconsciously sabotages his or her own success by doing something that will prevent that success. People experiencing this syndrome feel uncomfortable when things are going well, so they sabotage the whole situation in order to return to the low self-esteem identity to which they have become accustomed. A self-fulfilling prophecy exists when a person believes that something will happen, and because of this belief, that person acts in a way that makes the belief come true. In other words, if you feel you will fail, you act in a way that ensures failure.

There are other self-sabotaging patterns abuse victims adopt. It is not uncommon for victims of abuse to establish inappropriate relationships. Victims may also become crisis-oriented. Their reality can be so chaotic that they thrive on fixing everything for everyone else. Often, those who have been abused experience unresolved anger and have a tendency to erupt suddenly in anger at inconsequential events. This behavior is a signpost that there is a deeply sensitive, hurting place in the abused person's life. .

Abuse is difficult to deal with, especially when it is part of domestic violence, as the victim tries to survive, carrying old baggage, the mate, and societal perceptions. Society contributes to domestic violence by not taking it seriously enough and by treating it as expected, normal, or deserved. Society perpetuates domestic abuse in the following ways:

- Police may not treat domestic abuse as a crime, but rather as a domestic dispute.

- Courts may not award severe consequences, such as imprisonment or economic sanctions.

- A community usually doesn't ostracize domestic abusers.

- Clergy or counselors may have the attitude that the relationship will improve given more time and effort, even though all else indicates it will not.

- People may have the attitude that the abuse is the victim's fault, or that abuse is a normal part of marriage or domestic partnership.

- Gender-role socialization and stereotypes condone abusive behavior by men.

Throughout our lives, we are involved in many different kinds of relationships. We have friendships, romances, work and school-related connections, and familial ties. Each of these relationships has the potential to enrich us, adding to our feelings of self-worth, enjoyment, and growth. These relationships are healthy.

Trying Till I Get It Right

Halle was a natural performer, earning a handful of beauty pageant titles during the early 1980s, including Miss Teen Ohio and Miss Teen America. In 1983, when she was only seventeen years old, Halle's boyfriend at the time entered her name in the Miss Teen Ohio beauty pageant. Once again, it was no surprise that Halle got to wear the crown in that competition. She was eventually awarded first runner-up in the 1985 Miss USA competition. In addition, Halle won many other high-profile competitions.

Once she was done raking in points by winning pageant after pageant, in 1986, Halle began to pursue an education at Cleveland's Cuyahoga Community College, studying broadcast journalism. She attended college but abandoned her idea of a career in news reporting before receiving her degree. She chose to devote her time wholeheartedly to a career in entertainment. Halle moved to Chicago where she found work as a catalog model.

On her way to the top, Halle found herself unemployed in one of the most expensive cities in the country but soon landed a job on *Living Dolls*. The aspiring actress had begun a career in television. She was enjoying her new success, but it was overwhelming. One day she collapsed on the set. She was rushed to the hospital, where she was diagnosed as having diabetes. The show, *Living Dolls*, was about four struggling models. Halle played Emily Franklin in this unsuccessful spin-off from Tonya Danza's *Who's the Boss?* Unfortunately the ratings were not high enough to continue airing the show, and it was cancelled after three months.

Halle next appeared as Debbie Porter on *Knots Landing* in 1991, which was one of television's most-watched nighttime soaps. Television was good to Halle, but she wanted the big screen. She wanted the more challenging roles film had to offer and in 1993 landed the role of Queen in the Alex Halley miniseries *Queen*.

Halle's first role in a movie almost did not happen. She was hired to star in the comedy *Strictly Business*, but she was immediately fired by the director because she wasn't "black enough!" Halle was outraged, but when the director himself was fired, she was rehired by his replacement (USA Weekend, 2001).

Audiences took to Halle, and producers kept her busy. She landed a significant part in *The Last Boy Scout*. She then starred in a series of mostly lighthearted films, like *Boomerang, The Program*, and *Fatherhood*. But Halle didn't want to be seen as just window dressing. Her portrayal of a crack addict in Spike Lee's *Jungle Fever* won her critical acclaim, and she proved to be an effective dramatic lead opposite Jessica Lange in the heartwarming drama *Losing Isaiah*. Both films dealt with the kinds of racial insults Halle had to deal with her whole life.

With a few films completed, Halle accepted more offbeat roles, making a cameo performance in the film *CB4*, which traced the rise and fall of the titled rap group. The 1994 live-action version of *The Flintstones* featured Halle as a Stone Age seductress. Later that year, Halle was cast as the first African American to play the Queen of Sheba in Showtime's movie, *Solomon & Sheba*.

Halle's other credits included two 1996 crime thrillers, *The Rich Man's Wife* and *Executive Decision*, which marked her first leading role in a feature. She played one of three wives laying claim to Frankie Lymon's estate in the 1998 biographical drama, *Why Do Fools Fall in Love*, and she played a liberal urban youth in the political satire *Bulworth*, opposite Hollywood veteran Warren Beatty.

In 1999, Halle released a project she felt most passionate about, coproducing and starring in *Introducing Dorothy Dandridge*, an HBO biopic. Halle was noted for her striking resemblance to the late Dandridge and for her engaging depiction of the actress struggling to succeed in the racially biased industry of 1950s Hollywood. Halle earned both a Golden Globe award and an Emmy award for best actress in a television movie for that role.

Halle was featured in *X-Men*, the big-budget screen adaptation of the long-running Marvel comic. Halle's character, Storm, teamed with fellow mutant heroes, played by Anna Paquin and Patrick Stewart. In the summer of 2001, she costarred with John Travolta in an action movie, *Swordfish*. The publicity from this movie centered around Halle's topless scene.

Halle garnered the most positive critical notice of her film career in late 2001, for her performance as the wife of a death row prisoner, played by Sean "Puffy" Combs, who becomes romantically involved with a racist prison guard, played by Billy Bob Thornton, in the drama, *Monster's Ball*. The role earned Halle a Golden Globe for best actress in a drama and the Academy Award for best actress.

Halle's booming popularity led her to a multimillion dollar contract with Revlon. This contract has helped her gain worldwide recognition by putting her face in a series of eye-catching print ads. But no matter how good she looks, Halle would like her fans to see her outer beauty as a reflection of her inner beauty.

Halle's popularity was definitely a boost to her self-esteem, but maintaining that level was difficult and necessary. Self-esteem is important to a person's well being. It is the opinion you have of yourself and is based on your attitude about yourself as a person of value, your career achievements, and your perception of your purpose in life and place in the world. It defines your potential for success, your strengths and weaknesses, and your social status, and it affects how you relate to others.

People with normal self-esteem might doubt themselves from time to time, but their sense of self-worth consistently reverts back to a balanced state. Having healthy self-esteem does not mean feeling perfect. It means not having to consistently doubt yourself.

People with poor self-esteem often rely on how they are doing in the present to determine how they feel about themselves. They need positive external experiences to counteract the negative feelings and thoughts that constantly plague them.

Healthy self-esteem is based on our ability to assess ourselves for what we really are and still love ourselves unconditionally. This means being able to realistically acknowledge our strengths and weaknesses while, at the same time, accepting ourselves as worthwhile without conditions or reservations.

Our self-esteem develops and evolves throughout our lives as we build images of ourselves through our experiences with different people and activities. Experiences during our childhood play a particularly large role in shaping our self-esteem. How we were treated by the members of our family, our teachers, coaches, religious authorities, and peers contribute to the development of our basic self-esteem.

Our past experiences, even the ones we don't want to remember, are all alive and active in our daily lives, in the form of an inner voice. For people with healthy self-esteem, the messages from the inner voice are positive and reassuring. For people with low self-esteem, the inner voice becomes a harsh inner critic, constantly criticizing and belittling. Halle needed constant external success to counteract her inner voice. Her confidence was high after each success, but she always needed more.

It's Starting to Click

By delivering a powerful performance in *Monster's Ball*, Halle proved she was more than just a beauty. She was now being taken seriously and could pick her roles without worrying about the feedback. She pursued this new power by going after various types of roles. Halle accepted the role of Jinx in the twentieth James Bond feature, *Die Another Day*, opposite Pierce Brosnan as Agent 007. She was the first A-list, Oscar-winning Bond girl in a generation. She held her own in the film, causing the studio to take notice. After completing that role, she segued to *X2*, the sequel to *X-Men*, in which she reprised her role as Storm. Her most recent films include *House of Wax, Gothika, Robots* (voiced), *Their Eyes Were Watching God*, and *X-Men 3*.

Life has changed for Halle, thanks largely to *Monster's Ball*. As soon as Halle read the script, she knew she wanted the part. She called her agent enthusiastically and was surprised to hear that she was not being considered for the part. The producer of Monster's Ball did not feel she could deliver the character in the way he imagined the character to be. Her glamour almost kept her from getting the part. The director did not feel she would go along with the passionate love scene scripted for the picture.

Director Marc Forster wasn't sure Halle was prepared to go as far as he wanted. More precisely, he wondered about Halle's and Thornton's ability to portray an extremely gritty and intimate love scene. He was concerned whether Halle was willing to be naked. He wanted to have a raw love scene, and he wasn't sure if she'd be comfortable doing that. But Halle accepted, and she did what she had to do to deliver the part as the director intended.

She knew she had made it. Validation in the form of nominations and awards started rolling in, proving the she was the best of the best. This was all she thought she needed to heal her damaged self-esteem. But external boosts to one's self-esteem are always temporary, as she would eventual realize. Self-esteem is the fundamental essence that supports everything about you. It is built on self-acceptance and self-concept. Self-acceptance is basic and primitive and is shared by most living things. Self-acceptance is unconditional and is required before self-esteem can develop. Self-acceptance is not a denial of a need for change, improvement, or evolution. It is simply the recognition of what and who you are. This does not mean that if you have self-acceptance you cannot change and become better. You can. We all strive for perfection, not meaning to reach it, but using it as a motivator.

Nothing is more important to your existence than what you think of yourself. Everything you feel, think, and do is influenced by how you evaluate yourself, and this self-evaluation affects how you relate to others and who you have relationships with. People will come and people will go, but you will always have a relationship with yourself. Life is a journey. At the end of each trip you take, you will always be greeted by your self, as you are. It is unescapable.

Moving with Caution

With everything she had accomplished, there would always be hurdles, as there are for all of us. One of her biggest hurdles began the night of February 23, 2000, when the Golden Globe—winning actress ran her rented car into another car. Halle received a gash in her forehead, which required more than twenty stitches. The other driver's attorney was quick to point out that his client had suffered a broken wrist and neck and was experiencing back pain, and that firefighters had to pull her from the wreckage of her car.

Even now Halle can't remember what happened. The collision isn't just a blur; she has no memory of it. Although she has tried repeatedly to recall what happened, she says she doesn't have a clue how she went from driving to her friend's house to being a "bloody mess with a crashed car." Halle has accepted the judgment of doctors that because of the head injury she suffered in the accident, she may never remember. She acknowledges that she did leave the crash site before authorities arrived, and that is why, she says, she agreed to plead no contest to a misdemeanor charge of leaving the scene of a traffic accident (USA Weekend,2001).

Until the misdemeanor charge was issued, Halle says her life was "a living hell." For one thing, she realized there was the real possibility she would face felony hit-and-run charges and go to jail. For another, while authorities investigated the accident, she became the target of a rumor mill that charged her with everything from driving under the influence of alcohol and drugs to being involved in other hit-and-run accidents. These allegations were thoroughly investigated and found to be untrue.

More than anyone, Halle knows how incredible her total lack of recall seems. "I know people find it hard to believe because I couldn't believe it, and it happened to me," she says, referring not just to the accident but to the fact that she drove herself home afterward. She was not sure what had happened and had no answers as to why it had happened. She would sit for hours and hours hoping and praying that something would jog her memory."

Halle was placed on three years' probation and ordered to pay $13,500 in fines and penalties after pleading no contest to a misdemeanor charge of leaving the scene of a traffic accident. The judge also ordered the actress to perform 200 hours of community service and to make restitution as determined by the outcome of civil litigation arising from the accident (USA Weekend, 2001).

Those days of waiting to know her fate were horrible. She couldn't eat or sleep. She withdrew and did not want to face the pressures of her life. In the weeks following the accident, she learned a lot about the people around her, and she learned far more about herself. Some of these lessons were painful and life-changing. She knew that the accident was only a part of her troubles. She knew that she had to start facing her fears: long-standing, deeply rooted, life-ruling fears, most of which centered around her fear of being abandoned. It goes back to her childhood and not having her father.

Her self-confidence had been shattered. She was once again that child who felt she would not be accepted. She had no self-confidence. Self-confident people trust their own abilities. They have a general sense of control in their lives and believe that, within reason, they will be able to do what they wish, plan, and expect. But she felt none of this. She had lost her sense of control. She would later move past this incident and rebuild her confidence.

She thought the public would abandon her and that she would lose everything she had worked so hard for. She thought Eric Benét, whom she planned to wed at that time, would abandon her. But he showed her just how much he loved her. He was there for her throughout her hardships even though they would divorce later.

Reality Testing

Halle learned most of her lessons from her relationships with others. She learned from her interactions at a very young age. Society was her teacher. Her schoolmates were her adversaries, and men tried to make her into a victim. She took these painful experiences and grew into a strong woman to be reckoned with. Although her final lessons may yet be learned, she has reached a point in her life where she can look into the mirror and see a reflection of someone she can be proud of. On her way to developing this self image, she gained these insights:

Being thought of as "a beautiful woman" has spared me nothing in life. No heartache, no trouble. Beauty is essentially meaningless.

"I respond well to tortured characters. There's a place in me that can really relate to being the underdog."

"I think it's always best to be who you are."

"I know that there is a God—the God within me that's always present and will protect me."

"I'm not afraid to climb any mountain, because I know that I'm protected. Even if I fall and die, I'm still protected. My faith is on that level."

"I'm still a work in progress, but I know that as long as I stay close to God I'll be all right."

"I understand now that 'special love' exists between two people when the passions lie beneath the surface."

There's a place in me that can really relate to being the underdog. I'm always fighting to overcome the obstacle. I can really understand what's that about.

I'm really comfortable with who I am now, and not so much in need of the approval of other people like I used to be, and so I'm learning to look the other way.

I think sometimes it's hard for people to see past the physical. But honestly I could think of worst problems to have. I think it's harder being a black woman in this industry than looking the way I do. Yes, I think it's harder being a black woman than being considered beautiful.

My Way

Halle had a path paved with one obstacle after another, usually provided by people from whom she sought for love and comfort. The biggest obstacle, herself, would be her strongest adversary, one she would eventually have to face. And she did. Through the conflicts she has had with herself, Halle Berry has become a strong, empowered woman. From the time she was a young girl, Halle knew she would do extraordinary things. She had a clue that her good looks and charming personality would help define what these things would be. So she took her assets and turned then into accomplishments.

11

Enlightenment from The Wizard of Oz

Dorothy (aka Demi) lived in the great Kansas prairie with Uncle Henry, who was a farmer, and Aunt Em, who was his wife, and Toto, the family dog. Their house had a storm cellar where they could go during fierce windstorms.

One day, Uncle Henry sat on the doorstep and looked anxiously at the sky, which was grayer than usual. From the far north he heard a low wail of the wind. "There's a cyclone coming, Em!" he called to his wife. "Quick, Demi!" she screamed. "Run for the cellar!" Toto jumped out of Demi's arms and hid under the bed, and the girl started to get him. Aunt Em, badly frightened, threw open the trap door in the floor and climbed down the ladder into the small, dark hole. Demi caught Toto and started to follow her aunt. When she was halfway across the room, there came a great shriek from the wind, and the house shook so hard that she lost her footing and fell down on the floor.

The house whirled around two or three times and rose slowly through the air. Demi felt as if she were going up in a balloon.

The cyclone picked up the house then sat the house down very gently, for a cyclone, in the midst of a country of marvelous beauty.

Demi opened the door of the house and stood looking eagerly at the strange and beautiful sights, she noticed a group of the queerest people she had ever seen coming toward her. They were not as big as grown folk, but neither were they very small.

"You are welcome, most noble Sorceress, to the land of the Munchkins," said one of them. "We are so grateful to you for having killed the Wicked Witch of the East, and for setting our people free from bondage."

Demi said, with hesitation, "You are very kind, but there must be some mistake. I have not killed anything."

The Good Witch of the North appeared and explained to Demi that she had killed the bad witch. Demi noticed beautiful red shoes sticking out from underneath the house, which had landed on the wicked witch. The silver shoes are yours, and you shall have them to wear," proclaimed Glenda, the Good Witch of the North. She reached down, picked up the shoes, and after shaking the dust out of them, handed them to Demi.

Demi explained that she was lost and wanted to go home.

"Then you must go to the Emerald City. Perhaps Oz will help you."

"The road to the City of Emeralds is paved with yellow brick," said the Witch, "so you cannot miss it. When you get to Oz, do not be afraid of him, but tell your story and ask him to help you. Good-bye, my dear."

After some time had passed on her journey, Demi came upon a scarecrow who could talk.

"My name is Demi and I am going to the Emerald City to ask the great Oz to send me back to Kansas.

"Where is the Emerald City?" the scarecrow inquired. "And who is Oz?"

"Why, don't you know?" she returned, in surprise

"No, indeed. I don't know anything. You see, I am stuffed, so I have no brains at all," he answered sadly.

"Oh," said Demi. "I'm awfully sorry for you."

"Do you think," he asked, "if I go to the Emerald City with you, that Oz would give me some brains?"

"I cannot tell," she returned, "but you may come with me, if you like. If Oz will not give you any brains, you will be no worse off than you are now."

They began to head toward the Emerald City. Sometime later on their journey, she was startled to hear a deep groan nearby.

"What was that?" she asked timidly.

"I cannot imagine," replied the scarecrow, "but we can go and see."

One of the big trees had been partly chopped through, and standing beside it, with an uplifted ax in his hands, was a man made entirely of tin. His head and arms and legs were jointed upon his body, but he stood perfectly motionless, as if he could not stir at all.

"Did you groan?" asked Demi.

"Yes," answered the tin man, "I did. I've been groaning for more than a year, and no one has ever heard me before or come to help me."

"What can I do for you?" she inquired softly, for she was moved by the sad voice in which the man spoke.

"Get an oil can and oil my joints," he answered. "They are rusted so badly that I cannot move them at all. If I am well oiled, I shall soon be all right again. You will find an oil can on a shelf in my cottage."

Demi ran back to the cottage at once and found the oil can; then she returned and asked anxiously, "Where are your joints?"

She oiled the tin man who began to walk with them. While they were walking through the forest, the tin woodsman told the following story:

"I was born the son of a woodsman who chopped down trees in the forest and sold the wood for a living. When I grew up, I too became a woodchopper, and after my father died, I took care of my old mother as long as she lived. Then I made up my mind that, instead of living alone, I would marry, so that I might not become lonely.

"One of the Munchkin girls was so beautiful that I soon grew to love her with all my heart. She, on her part, promised to marry me as soon as I could earn enough money to build a better house for her. Thereupon, the wicked witch enchanted my ax, and when I was chopping away at my best one day, for I was anxious to get the new house and my wife as soon as possible, the ax slipped all at once and cut off my left leg. Then it cut off my right leg, my left arm, and my right arm. But I replaced them.

"I thought I had beaten the wicked witch, and so I worked harder than ever; but little did I know how cruel my enemy could be. She thought of a new way to kill my love for the beautiful Munchkin maiden. She made my ax slip again so that it cut right through my body, splitting me into two halves. But, alas! I now had no heart, so I lost all my love for the Munchkin girl and did not care whether I married her or not. I suppose she is still waiting for me to come after her. I will ask Oz for a heart."

"All the same," said the scarecrow, "I shall ask for brains instead of a heart, for a fool would not know what to do with a heart if he had one."

"I shall take the heart," returned the tin Woodsman, "for brains do not make one happy, and happiness is the best thing in the world."

As they were walking on, they heard a terrible roar. The next moment, a great lion bounded into the road in front of them. Little Toto ran barking toward the lion, and the great beast had opened his mouth to bite the dog when Demi, fearing Toto would be killed and heedless of danger, rushed forward and slapped the lion on his nose as hard as she could, crying out, "Don't you dare to bite Toto! You ought to be ashamed of yourself, a big beast like you, trying to bite a poor little dog!"

The lion began to cry and admitted he was a coward. "I suppose I was born that way. All the other animals in the forest naturally expect me to be brave, for the lion is everywhere thought to be the king of beasts. I learned that if I roared very loudly, every living thing was frightened and got out of my way. Whenever

I've met a man, I've been awfully scared, but I have just roared and men have always run away as fast as they could go. But that doesn't make me any braver, and as long as I know myself to be a coward, I shall be unhappy."

It was suggested that the lion join them to ask for courage. So they started for Oz and finally reached the great wizard, who had no powers.

"Can't you give me brains?" asked the scarecrow.

"You don't need them. You are learning something every day. A baby has brains, but it doesn't know much. Experience is the only thing that brings knowledge, and the longer you are on earth the more experience you are sure to get."

"That may all be true," said the scarecrow, "but I shall be very unhappy unless you give me brains."

The false wizard looked at him carefully. He then gave the scarecrow a diploma.

"Oh, thank you—thank you!" cried the scarecrow. "I'll find a way to use them, never fear!"

"But how about my courage?" asked the lion anxiously.

"You have plenty of courage, I am sure," answered Oz. "All you need is confidence in yourself. There is no living thing that is not afraid when it faces danger. The true courage is in facing danger when you are afraid, and that kind of courage you have in abundance."

"Perhaps I have, but I'm scared just the same," said the lion. "I shall really be very unhappy unless you give me the sort of courage that makes one forget he is afraid."

And so the lion received a medal of courage to prove that his courage did exist.

"How about my heart?" asked the tin woodsman.

"Why ask for that?" answered Oz. "I think you are wrong to want a heart. It makes most people unhappy. If you only knew it, you are in luck not to have a heart."

"That must be a matter of opinion," said the tin woodsman. "For my part, I will bear all the unhappiness without a murmur, if you will give me the heart." And Oz gave the tin man a beating mechanical heart.

"And now," said Demi, "how am I to get back to Kansas?"

"If Demi would only be content to live in the Emerald City," continued the scarecrow, "we might all be happy together."

"But I don't want to live here," cried Demi. "I want to go to Kansas, and live with Aunt Em and Uncle Henry."

"I think I should like to go back to Kansas" said Dorothy.

A bright light appeared in front of Dorothy. A woman in a white gown stepped out of the light proclaiming to be the good witch.

"The silver shoes," said the good witch, "have wonderful powers."

Demi now took Toto up solemnly in her arms, and having said one last good-bye, she clapped the heels of her shoes together three times, saying, "Take me home to Aunt Em!"

The next thing she said was "good gracious," for she was sitting on the broad Kansas prairie, and just before her was the new farmhouse Uncle Henry had built after the cyclone had carried away the old one. Uncle Henry was milking the cows in the barnyard, and Toto had jumped out of her arms and was running toward the barn, barking furiously.

Aunt Em had just come out of the house to water the cabbages when she looked up and saw Demi running toward her.

"My darling child!" she cried, folding the little girl in her arms and covering her face with kisses. "Where in the world did you come from?"

"From the land of Oz," said Demi gravely. "And here is Toto, too. And oh, Aunt Em! I'm so glad to be at home again!"

Many feel that there is always something better out there. Usually when we venture out, we always want to go back home, even if only for a short while. There is truly, for most, no place like home. A house is a building; a home is a state of mind. Those who can happily say, "There's no place like home" feel fortunate. But what about those who come from homes they have had to escape or those who never knew what "home" is like? What happens to them?

We applaud the good witch. We like to see good triumphing over evil again and again. We like to believe that good will always prevail. It makes it easier for us to survive the hard times. If we believe the good in ourselves, we believe that we will prevail, but along with the good there needs to be determination and perseverance.

Rising above yourself is helping others even in times when you are troubled. Demi knew this and acted on it. "Misery likes company" is an idea that is only too familiar. Many people who are having a hard time feel better if someone is having a hard time with them; so they don't bother to help others but instead feed the misery of others. In this tale, though, Demi shows much empathy and rises above her own concerns to help others. When people bond with others in an effort to help, they often find happiness.

Everyone wants to be intelligent. What does this mean? In book sense, being intelligent means having a good memory and being able to think logically. If you have these strengths but lack the experience and the ability to learn from your experiences, you will have weapons you don't know how best to use. Intelligence is also using what you have learned from your experiences in life. It is believing in yourself and taking your talents and making things happen.

To have a heart is to show compassion and empathy toward others. Your relationships will define whether you have a heart and what your heart is made of. Having a heart can be shown in many ways. Usually it involves being good to others and to yourself. No matter what the outcome of your achievements, if they were done with malice, they were not done with a good heart and therefore mean nothing.

Courage is so often misunderstood. Sometimes courage involves backing away and turning the other cheek. Sometimes courage is facing life's challenges with faith and hope. Courage is giving yourself to others with full faith as you face life's challenges.

12

Demi Moore: A Duchess's Determination

"It's how we choose to deal with those things that happen in our lives
that matters."
—Demi Moore

Unvalued Doll

Demetria Gene Guynes, now known as Demi Moore, was born on November
11, 1962, in Roswell, New Mexico. She was raised in a poor family that was constantly on the move. Demi's biological father was an Air Force serviceman. Demi
never really knew her biological father, who left her mother, Virginia, months
before Demi was born. Demi grew up believing that her stepfather, Danny

Guynes, was her biological father. He treated her as his daughter, and she had his last name. As a teenager, she was shocked to learn the truth about Danny Guynes; although he was the man who stepped in when her real father left her mother, he was not her biological father.

Demi was born in a trailer park. Her stepfather, a salesman who sold advertising space for newspapers, was frequently unemployed. He was a heavy drinker and so was her mother. They were poor. When they did have money, it was wasted on gambling and alcohol. Demi had a deprived and chaotic childhood. Most of it was shrouded in poverty, alcohol, and domestic abuse.

Her stepfather was an unstable character, who contributed to her complicated childhood. Her mother and stepfather fought and drank constantly. They were physically and emotionally abusive to one another. Domestic violence was a constant state in their home.

Domestic violence affects basic needs children have to experience safety, trust, control, intimacy, and a connection to others. When these needs are met, people feel safe. They have a solid sense of self. They feel capable of taking control of their world. In doing so, they are able to participate intimately with others. When basic needs are not met, people feel vulnerable, betrayed, flawed, fearful, incompetent, disconnected, and alienated.

When people's needs are not met, they may view the world as dangerous and threatening. They feel vulnerable to harm, believing that others and the world around them are not trustworthy or reliable. They go through life believing that others will exploit and control them. This makes them feel that it is too risky to participate intimately with others. They instead turn to dysfunctional ways of dealing with the world. Often they are aggressive and may use alcohol or drugs to feel less vulnerable. Children raised in violent and abusive homes have a higher risk of abusing alcohol and drugs, as well as a higher risk of delinquency.

Demi and her brother witnessed continual violence between their mother and father. Although the aggression was not directed at them, they were a part of it. They heard the conflicts in the form of anger and discord, which became regular parts of their environment. Their home was rarely peaceful; instead, it was a constant battleground of domestic violence.

Children don't have to be physically or verbally abused to be hurt by domestic violence. Hearing or seeing the abuse of one parent by the other takes a huge toll on them. As a result, children may

- Develop psychological difficulties which last a lifetime
- Grow up believing violence is a normal part of family life

- Live in daily fear of what to expect at home
- Be filled with chaos and tension, making it difficult to trust others
- Feel responsible for the abuse and powerless to stop it

Demi and her biological brother were neglected in the process, partly as a result of alcohol abuse in the home, and partly as a result of poverty. Demi's environment was full of abuse and neglect. Demi and her brother were not abused directly, but they were neglected. The neglect was of an emotional nature. Emotional neglect includes such actions as chronic or extreme spousal abuse in the child's presence, refusal or failure to provide needed psychological care, and constant belittling and withholding of affection.

Demi and her brother experienced some of these actions. Experiencing this pattern of behavior can lead to poor self-image, alcohol or drug abuse, destructive behavior, and even suicide. Demi's stepfather and mother kept on drinking, arguing, and beating one another, until her stepfather left. He later committed suicide, adding another abusive element to her childhood. She was seventeen years old when her stepfather died.

Nomadic Chaos

When Demi was a child, she would travel like a nomad from town to town while her stepfather, employed as a newspaper ad salesman, looked for a job. "There were bad times in my childhood. There were some really good times in there as well. I wasn't afforded the luxury to live with the idea that it was painful or fearful, because I needed to only be strong, so I could survive." Her stepfather, Danny Guynes, did not provide much stability in her life. He frequently changed jobs and made the family move frequenlty while Demi was growing up (Goodall, 27). This was not helpful in her developing into a strong stable individual. Her stepfather regularly lost or walked out on jobs and moved his family dozens of times from one home and neighborhood to another. The difficulty adjusting to new environments was compounded by the dysfunctional, abusive relationship between Demi's mother and stepfather.

Demi stated that by moving a lot she learned how to assimilate herself into whatever new surrounding she was in. She became comfortable with people quickly. She felt that this was one of the strongest contributing factors to her becoming an actor, because she constantly had to adjust, and even reinvent herself.

But moving also made it difficult for her to become attached to people because she knew she would soon have to leave them. "I learned to enjoy people and the places for the time I had, for the moment, to be in the moment, and to move on"(Rubenstein, 1996).

Moving to a new community may be one of the most stress-producing experiences a family faces. Frequent moves, or even a single move, can be especially hard on children and adolescents. Moves interrupt friendships. When a child moves to a new neighborhood, that child is the new kid on the block. New children in the neighborhood often feel that everyone has made their friends and there is no place for them to fit in. At the beginning, it seems that everyone else has a best friend or is securely involved with a group of peers. This is a stressful situation for a child.

The older the child, the more difficult the move is because of the increasing importance of friends and peer group. Children find it difficult to express how they feel, especially if they feel powerless to affect the outcome. Some may not talk about their distress. Loved ones should be aware of warning signs of depression related to moving.

The more frequently a family moves, the more important is the need for internal stability. This was not the case with Demi's family. There was no stability in her home. The chaos within her home matched the external confusion caused by the frequent moves.

Moving can be a positive experience for children with the proper support from parents, leading to increased self-confidence and interpersonal skills. Although Demi lacked support from her parents, she made the best of a difficult life and turned potentially negative experiences into positive lessons upon which she would build her acting career.

Most of Demi's needs were not met as a child. She did not feel safe or secure. There was constant conflicts and confusion in her household. There was no stability. The family moved constantly, making her environment and future unpredictable. Where there is no predictability, there is no security. Demi didn't know whether she would wake up in the same home with parents coexisting peacefully, or in a new home with parents who were ready to kill one another. She never felt safe or secure.

Safety needs translate into security needs. To be safe, you need to be able to count on stability, dependability, protection, and freedom from fear, anxiety, and chaos. You need structure, order, law, limits, and a strong protector(s). Demi's protectors, her parents, were too weak to offer any type of security.

Meeting safety needs results from establishing stability and consistency in a chaotic world. These needs are mostly psychological in nature. We need the security of a home and family. However, if a family is dysfunctional (i.e., with an alcoholic parent), it is difficult for children to concentrate on anything else because they are constantly concerned for their safety. Love and belongingness have to wait until they feel safe.

Demi and her brother found it difficult to feel safe in an environment that was unpredictable. They did what they could to cope with their environment. They were determined to survive the situation into which they had been born. The safety and security most children felt while growing up was absent in Demi's home.

A child feels safe when there is some kind of undisrupted routine or rhythm. In a home with alcoholism, nothing is routine. The alcoholic acts impulsively, pulling everyone in the home into an unpredictable existence. Children develop best in a predictable, lawful, orderly world. Inconsistency on the part of parents makes a child feel anxious and unsafe. This treatment is threatening, and makes the world look unreliable, unsafe, or unpredictable. People thrive better under a system that has at least a skeletal outline of a routine. There needs to be something that can be counted on, not only for the present but also for the future. People, especially children, need an organized and structured world rather than an unorganized or unstructured one. Parents have a central role in providing this structure.

Demi's parents, although immersed in their own problems, cared for their children in an unhealthy way. Unhealthy in that their care was neglectful and given in a hostile and chaotic environment. One minute the care was shrouded in hostility, the next moment in love. This unhealthy display of love is sometimes perceived as lack of love. This type of love is usually harmful, causing emotional turmoil in the one toward whom it is directed. We need to feel loved by others, to be accepted by others. We need to be needed. Having affectionate relations with other people, especially with parents, is a must.

In addition to needing a caring connection to others, we need to be respected and seen as valuable. We all have a need or desire for self-respect and self-esteem. Developing healthy self-esteem is a direct result of environment. Self-esteem may result from competence or mastery of a task, or it may develop when there's attention and recognition from others. Everyone needs to feel appreciated and wanted. There wasn't much in Demi's environment to be proud of. There wasn't much there for her to use to develop healthy self-esteem.

Demi reports that, when she was young, she didn't have a lot of self-esteem. Demi was a quiet withdrawn child, visibly nervous and unsettled (Goodall, 24). To fit in she looked to her environment for clues she could not find within herself. She once described herself as a skinny, bespectacled, cross-eyed, clumsy ugly duckling. Her hair was cut like a boy's. She was nerdy. She stated that "Even when I blossomed in other ways, there's that feeling that you still carry around (Goodall, 24).

High self-esteem leads to feelings of self-confidence, self-worth, strength, capability, and adequacy, a sense of being useful and necessary in the world. Deficiency in basic emotional needs produces feelings of inferiority, weakness, and helplessness. It is hard for an individual with low self-esteem to look at the future with encouragement, since this individual may feel he or she is not worthy of a prosperous and happy future.

As long as we are motivated to satisfy self-esteem needs, we are moving toward growth, and toward self-actualization. Satisfying needs such as security, self-esteem, love and belonging, is healthy. Blocking gratification which can come from the above makes us sick. We all have needs that must be satisfied and should be satisfied; otherwise we become sick.

The little security Demi had was in knowing that she had a mother and a father. This was shattered when she found out that the man she had thought was her father was actually her stepfather. She discovered the truth in her early teens while rifling through her mother's personal papers. This truth hit her hard. She viewed it as a betrayal by her mother and other family members who had known and had covered up the truth. She went in search of the truth while visiting an aunt in Texas.

Her father, Charles Harmon, an Air Force officer, had married and left her mother all in the space of two months. He had tried to make contact when he heard of Demi's birth, but her mother refused to let him into her life. He had never seen his daughter and didn't know what she looked like until he visited her briefly at her aunt's house. When she met her real father, Demi did not feel a connection. Demi described the meeting as a bizarre experience, one she never repeated.

And as if this wasn't enough, the father who had raised her committed suicide when Demi was sixteen by inhaling carbon monocide fumes from the exhaust of his car (Goodall, 30). This was, around the time she discovered who her real father was. His suicide confused Demi. Why had he given up? There were so many unanswered questions. Dealing with the suicide of a family member is confusing and traumatic, and there are many emotions associated with such a tragedy.

Shock is the first reaction. One feels numb for a while. When one feels numb, one is unable to follow a normal routine. However, the numbness protects the individual from feeling the full extent of what has happened until the mind has a chance to adjust and accept the situation. Thus, shock can be healthy, protecting one from the initial pain of the loss, helping one get through the loss.

After the initial shock, one may feel angry, guilty, and sad. These feelings may be overwhelming and confusing. Initially one may handle the feelings well, only to have them return for no apparent reason. These feelings, and the confusion and helplessness that come with them, gradually pass.

One feels angry for many reasons. Anger is often directed at the deceased: how could he or she have done this? The anger may be self-directed, a feeling that one should have noticed that something was wrong and been able to stop it. The anger is a natural consequence of the hurt and rejection one feels. If the anger is denied, it will eventually come out in other ways that may be destructive and that will prolong the healing process. Anger toward the deceased is normal when the manner of death is suicide.

It is important to recognize anger directed at oneself. This anger is closely linked with feelings of guilt. If the deceased was someone with regular close contact, the guilt will be intense. And if the death came as a complete surprise, it will leave everyone desperately searching for reasons why.

Which World Is Mine?

Demi moved with her mother to Los Angeles. She and her mother had a small apartment in West Hollywood. It was the first permanent home they had after living in trailer parks for so many years. But Demi wanted more. Demi was focused on the future, but her mother would prove to be a burden. He mother's drinking problem was so overwhelming that Demi wondered whether she would ever have the opportunity to act, or whether she would spend her time caring for her mother.

Demi went to school at Fairfax High in West Hollywood. It was difficult. She did not want to be there and found it nearly unbearable.She was sixteen years old when she quit school and began to pursue a modeling career as a pinup girl. She could see the wealth and opportunity the city of Los Angeles had to offer and was determined to get some of it for herself.

She agreed to pose for a photographer while wearing only a bathing suit. Her picture was chosen for the cover of *Oui* magazine, which was geared toward a male audience. The issue also included a full spread on Demi; however, this publicity did not provide the big break she had hoped for and needed.

The problems with her mother increased, and eventually her mother and Demi separated. Later, when Demi began to make money on a consistent basis, she bought a house in Hollywood and asked her mother and brother to move in with her. Things were looking up. Her mother, however, reported that she and her daughter were drinking and doing drugs heavily at this time. Demi had used Quaaludes, marijuana, and alcohol for years, and her drug use was becoming serious.

Her mother's attitudes and behavior contributed to Demi's substance use. Her mother was not a conventional parent. She had a criminal record, accompanied by alcohol and drug use. She had been arrested several times for drunk driving. Her record also included arson. Demi tried repeatedly to get help for her mother. She enrolled her mother in substance abuse treatment programs. When that didn't seem to work, Demi gave up and severed contact. This difficult relationship was accented by her mother's accusations that Demi was not taking care of her, accusations she made to the press. Demi's mother posing nude for *High Society* magazine in 1993 (Gunyes,1993), put an additional strain on their relationship.

Living with a nonrecovering alcoholic in the family can contribute to the stress felt by all members of the family. Each member may be affected differently. Not all families of alcoholics experience or react to this stress in the same way.

Children raised in alcoholic families have different life experiences than children raised in nonalcoholic families. They have problems and stressors that produce distorted perceptions and attitudes. Often these problems are carried into adulthood. Children of alcoholic families often seek relationships where they can recreate the roles that made them feel significant in their dysfunctional family, causing the dysfunction to follow them wherever they go. As they become adults, these children need to recognize this tendency in order to change the way they view the world and themselves so that they can break the cycle.

The roles played by the children of dysfunctional families make their behaviors incompatible with healthy relationships. They experience a family system in extreme chaos. Life in this environment is arbitrary, unpredictable, chaotic, and filled with double-bind messages and broken promises. When they enter into healthy relationships, they are confused and frustrated.

The reality of their world is defined by the abnormal behavior of their alcoholic parents, leaving children of alcoholics with difficulties in handling everyday tasks. These past experiences may cause them to

- Judge themselves harshly
- Have difficulty with intimate relationships
- Overreact to changes over which they have no control
- Have difficulty having fun
- Constantly seek approval and affirmation
- Guess at what normal behavior is
- Usually feel they are different from other people
- Become overly responsible or irresponsible
- Lie when it would be just as easy to tell the truth
- Be extremely loyal, even in the face of evidence that the loyalty is undeserved

Alcohol causes the environment to become unpredictable. The inability to predict, the stress of living in a chaotic existence where things just happen, causes individuals to be impulsive. They enter into courses of action without giving serious consideration to alternative behaviors or possible consequences. This impulsively leads to confusion, self-loathing, and loss of control over their environment. In addition, they spend an excessive amount of energy cleaning up the mess.

Alcoholism is a disease that affects not only the addicted person, but his or her family as well. Sometimes children of alcoholics are physically, sexually, and emotionally abused. But even if no overt abuse takes place, a child growing up in an alcoholic family suffers damage.

Demi adopted part of her mother's lifestyle: she started drinking alcohol as a way to cope with life's stressors. Her experience with her mother had taught her that this is what she should do when times got hard. In 1984, for example, she showed up intoxicated at a shooting of *St. Elmo's Fire*. At the wardrobe fitting, Demi was staggering and was clearly intoxicated. She was called into the office and was told she needed to clean up her act or she would be dropped from the film. She looked like a wreck. "The first week of rehearsals, I realized Demi had a serious problem with drugs and alcohol," recalls director Joel Schumacher. The studio wanted her released from the film, but Schumacher told her he'd give her one chance to check into rehab. She was advised to join an all-expense-paid residential drug treatment program. She agreed (Goodall, 41).

Children of alcoholics suffer psychologically, emotionally, and socially as a result of their experience in the alcoholic environment. They are forced to play roles and meet parental needs that children in other families are not. The role Demi played in *St. Elmo's Fire*, a confused individual who was abusing substances, mirrored her life. Demi was abusing drugs, mostly cocaine and alcohol. After director Joel Schumacher gave her a choice of being fired from the set of *St. Elmo's Fire* or helping herself, Demi began to turn her life around. The two-week drug rehab program helped her to return to work. She has remained clean and sober ever since.

After the rehab experience, Demi's life and career were looking up. This made her feel good about herself and gave her confidence and strength. But the baggage of her childhood weighed heavily on her self-esteem. She decided to go with the one thing she knew she could count on: her good looks and talent. She knew that her beauty was her greatest asset and would give her a chance for a better future.

Demi learned about empowerment at the rehab center. She realized the power within herself. If you are not aware of this power it is difficult to have high self esteem. Without it you are lost, at the mercy of others. Although self-esteem applies to every aspect of how you see yourself, it is often mentioned in terms of appearance or body image. Body image is how you perceive your body and how you feel about your physical appearance. We tend to relate self-esteem to body image for several reasons. First of all, most people care about how other people view them. Unfortunately, many people judge others by the clothes they wear, the shape of their bodies, or the way they wear their hair. Body image affects how people view themselves because our society is very conscious of physical appearance. Physical appearance is the first quality by which people are judged. If you feel attractive, you will act accordingly. If a person feels as if he or she looks different or worse than others, then body image and self-esteem may be affected negatively.

Demi's sense of self-esteem was highly influenced by her looks. Even in her late teens, she knew she was beautiful, but there was something she wanted to change. She was self-conscious about her slightly cross-eyed right eye. When she was able, she had surgery to fix her eye. She needed two surgeries to correct this problem.

There was an image Demi needed to project, not only for the public but for herself. If you have a positive body image, you probably like the way you look and accept yourself for the way you are. This is a healthy attitude that allows you to explore other aspects of life, such as increased independence, educational opportunities, and occupational goals. But if you become obsessed with your looks, this will interfere with your ability to focus on other things that are equally—or more—important.

There are things about yourself you can change and things you can't. You need to accept what you can't change. But if there are things about yourself that you do want to change and can, then make goals for yourself and proceed with caution and persistence. It is from your self-image that you develop labels for yourself, expectations for how you are to act, and goals for your future.

A Soapy Start

After completing rehab Demi found a new clarity in life and she began to take charge of her career. After becoming well known for her role on the soap opera *General Hospital*, Demi made the leap to the A-list of Hollywood stardom. Demi had success with *Ghost*, a supernatural romantic drama costarring Patrick Swayze and Whoopi Goldberg. She then acted in three straight critical flops: *Nothing But Trouble*, *The Butcher's Wife*, and *Mortal Thoughts*.

Over the next several years, Demi scored three straight box-office hits, beginning with the 1992 military courtroom drama, *A Few Good Men*, costarring Tom Cruise and Jack Nicholson. In 1993, she played a woman pursued by a wealthy tycoon, played by Robert Redford, in *Indecent Proposal*. The next year, Demi portrayed a sexually aggressive business executive harassing Michael Douglas in *Disclosure*.

The tide turned again in 1995. Demi's next several projects met with a harsh reception from critics and audiences alike. Both *The Scarlet Letter* and *The Juror* were flops. Although her $12.5 million paycheck for the 1996 *Striptease* was the highest salary ever paid an actress for a single movie at that time, the film did not do well. Demi received slightly better reviews for her role as a Navy SEAL in *G. I. Jane*, but the project failed to find commercial success. She had more luck as a producer, working on *If These Walls Could Talk*. She then produced two extremely successful Austin Powers movies, both starring Mike Myers.

In 1999, Demi signed a production deal with Miramax Films. The next year, she played dual roles in the romantic thriller, *Passion of Mind*. This was her first acting project since 1997. The film met with a mediocre reception.

Demi was then cast for *Charlie's Angels: Full Throttle*. She played the fallen angel, Madison Lee, a role for which she received almost as much attention as did the film's returning stars, Drew Barrymore, Cameron Diaz, and Lucy Liu.

Demi's daughters desperately wanted her to do the film. Everyone saw how stunning she looked in her bikini and knew she was worth what they paid her.

Although her films' popularity has varied, Demi's fans loved her. They repeatedly voted her top honors at the People's Choice Awards. But the critics have been hard on her. Demi has been criticized for being too demanding and controlling on her films, and her battles with directors and studios have been aired publicly.

Finding Myself within Myself

Demi has a lot to reflect on when looking back on her life experiences, both professionally and personally. In 1981, Demi married Freddy Moore, a rock musician. They were married after knowing each other for three months. Their marriage lasted only two years. The couple was known for their extravagant lifestyle.

It was at this time that Demi Moore launched her acting career, beating out a thousand other hopefuls to win a role on the daytime soap opera, *General Hospital*. She made several forgettable films (including *Parasite*) during her tenure on the popular soap, but she left the show when she won a supporting role in *Blame It on Rio*, a film starring Michael Caine. Demi starred in a few other, less successful movies during the next several years, including *About Last Night*, *Wisdom*, and *We're No Angels*.

At the beginning of her acting career Demi had entered into a phase of wild partying, drinking, and using drugs. She was running with the Hollywood crowd, becoming a second-generation alcoholic. She was young and did not know how to deal with her sudden burst of fame (on *General Hospital*) and turned to alcohol to cope.

Then came Emilio Estevez. The affair between Demi and Estevez started with the filming of *St. Elmo's Fire*. Demi's three-year relationship and on-again, off-again engagement with Estevez ended in 1987.

Shortly thereafter, Demi met actor Bruce Willis, then the star of the television show, *Moonlighting*. After an intense, three-month courtship, Demi and Bruce were married in November 1987.

In Bruce Willis, Demi had found someone she thought was her soul mate. She met him at a screening of Estevez's 1987 film, *Stakeout*. After seeing each other almost daily for the first few months, they were married in Vegas by Little Richard, and soon after, they started their family. They have three daughters, Rumer,

Scout, and Tallulah. "A family, for me as a young girl, was my image of what I hoped for. It was part of the big picture," Demi told *Vanity Fair* in 1992.

Demi sparked controversy when she appeared nude on the cover of *Vanity Fair* while she was pregnant with Scout. Demi stated that posing nude while pregnant was for her family. The photographer had taken pictures of her earlier. She knew how people would react and expected the controversy. "They don't want to embrace pregnancy and sensuality. They're afraid to imagine a pregnant woman as sexy"(Rubenstein, 1996).

"It's funny how when a child is born, it's this glorious moment in everyone's life, and you're the most wonderful woman that ever existed. But while you're pregnant, you're made to feel neither beautiful nor sexually viable. Women can either be sexy or be a mother. I didn't want to have to choose, so I challenged that. I'm not the only one."

Demi's first pregnancy allowed her to get off of the Hollywood merry-go-round. She concentrated on nothing but the upcoming birth of her child. She waited a year and a half before accepting another movie role. Bruce was very supportive during her pregnancy. Bruce was present and active during the birth, actually delivering the baby himself. The birth was filmed and has been viewed often by family and friends.

As the 1990s came to an end, the always-controversial Demi faced two difficult life-changing events in her personal life. In 1993, Demi's mother posed nude in *High Society* magazine, shocking Demi and the press. Clearly the relationship between Demi and her mother was falling apart. Demi had been paying her mother's bills and, at that point, cut her off. They later reconciled when Demi learned of her mother's cancerous brain tumor. Demi and her three daughters spent the last three months of her mother's life with her at her home in New Mexico. She was by her mother's side when she died at the age of fifty-four in 1998.

In June 1998, Demi and Bruce announced their separation after almost eleven years of marriage. Although they remained legally married for the next two years, the marriage was effectively over. Demi had to cope with the breakup of her marriage and the death of her mother.

In 1999, the ex-couple, along with fellow investors Arnold Schwarzenegger and Sylvester Stallone, were forced to file for bankruptcy protection for their restaurant chain, *Planet Hollywood*. Demi and Bruce were formally divorced in the fall of 2000. She continued to live on the couple's property in Hailey, Idaho, with her children, while Bruce lived nearby.

Demi and Ashton Kutcher married in 2005 in Los Angeles after a two-year-long relationship. Kutcher, whose break came as a star in television's *That 70s Show*, is cocreator of the MTV reality show, *Punk'd*. Kutcher wasted no time carving out a place in his life for Demi and her three daughters. They call him MOD, short for "My Other Dad."

A Twisty Winding Road

The roads Demi traveled changed often. She has had difficulty finding her way to solid ground. Although she grew up on a foundation that was shaky, she took it in stride. She learned how to adapt and cope with what life dished out. Demi learned strength and persistence on her way to a better life. These are some of the lessons which she learned during her journey.

It's how we choose to deal with those things that happen in our lives that matters.

"Marriage was a goal. A family, for me as a young girl, was my image of what I hoped for. It was part of the big picture."

"The truth is you can have a great marriage, but there are still no guarantees."

Success has to be an inside job. Happiness does not come from external material things. Even people don't make us ultimately happy.

"I want things to be the best they can be. I want greatness."

"I don't think I plan that far in advance. I try to focus on the present, what I'm doing now.

I feel like the best design I can have is an awareness of where I've come from so that I don't repeat myself.

"Happiness does not come from external material things. Even people don't make us ultimately happy."

Well, like many people, I think I'm my own worst critic. And I think I take a lot out in an internally abusive way, looking at how I measure up, which usually was never enough. I never, never was as good as someone else.

Home at Last

Demi hoped for the basics: a home and a family she could be safe with and call her own. Her dreams expanded. She used her assets to gain popularity and financial success. Demi found what she could call home, comprised of the children she loves and an accomplished career that helped her define herself and what her life would be. It was a long way from her beginnings to where she is now, but she dug her heels in and climbed over the obstacles—and never looked back.

13

The Glass Slipper: Cinderella's Lesson

Once there was a gentleman who remarried. His second wife was a proud, vain woman. She had two daughters of her own by a former marriage, who were also vain and proud. The man also had a daughter from a former marriage. His daughter was of unparalleled goodness and sweetness of temper. Her name was Cinderella.

No sooner were the ceremonies of the wedding over than the stepmother began to show her true colors. She could not bear the good qualities of her pretty stepdaughter, Cinderella, who made her daughters appear unattractive and odd. She employed Cinderella in the meanest work of the house. Cinderella slept in a sorry garret, on a wretched straw bed, while her sisters slept in fine rooms.

Poor Cinderella bore it all patiently, and dared not tell her father, who would have scolded her, for his wife governed him entirely.

In a kingdom nearby, it happened that the king's son gave a ball and invited all persons of fashion to it. Cinderella's stepsisters talked all day long of nothing but how they should dress for the ball. But Cinderella was not included. All alone, she began to cry. Her fairy godmother saw her all in tears and asked her what was the matter.

"I wish I could. I wish I could," sobbed Cinderella. She was not able to speak the rest.

Her fairy godmother said to her, "You wish that you could go to the ball; is it not so?"

"Yes," cried Cinderella, with a great sigh.

"Well," said her godmother, "be but a good girl, and I will arrange it so that you can go to the ball." Then she said to Cinderella, "Run into the garden and bring me a pumpkin."

Cinderella went immediately to gather the finest pumpkin she could find, and she brought it to her godmother. The godmother struck the pumpkin with her wand, and it was instantly turned into a fine coach, gilded all over with gold.

The godmother then found six mice and gave each mouse a little tap with her wand, and each mouse was that moment turned into a fine horse.

"But must I go in these nasty rags?" asked Cinderella.

Her godmother then touched her with her wand, and, at the same instant, Cinderella's clothes turned into cloth of gold and silver, all beset with jewels. This done, she gave Cinderella a pair of glass slippers, the prettiest in the whole world, and Cinderella got up into her coach.

Cinderella's godmother commanded her not to stay past midnight, telling her that if she stayed one moment longer, the coach would be a pumpkin again, her horses mice, her coachman a rat, her footmen lizards, and her clothes just as they were before.

Cinderella promised to leave the ball before midnight and then drove away, scarcely able to contain her joy. At the palace, the king's son, who had been told that a great princess whom nobody knew had arrived, ran out to receive her. He gave Cinderella his hand as she alighted from the coach, and he led her into the hall, among all the company. There immediately was a profound silence. Everyone stopped dancing, and the violins ceased to play; everyone was so entranced with the beauty of the unknown newcomer.

Nothing was heard but the whispers of people saying, "How beautiful she is! How beautiful she is!"

She danced so very gracefully that they all admired her. A fine meal was served, but the young prince ate not a morsel, so intently was he gazing at her.

The king's son was always by her side and never ceased his compliments and kind speeches to her. Cinderella forgot what her godmother had told her. She thought that it was no later than eleven when she counted the clock striking twelve. She jumped up and fled, as nimble as a deer. The prince followed but could not overtake her. She left behind one of her glass slippers, which the prince picked up most carefully. Cinderella reached home, quite out of breath and in her nasty old clothes, having nothing left of all her finery but one of the little slippers, the mate to the one that she had dropped.

The prince asked the guards at the palace gate if they had seen a princess go out. They replied that they had seen no one leave but a young girl, very shabbily dressed, who had more the air of a poor country wench than a gentlewoman.

The prince was very much in love with the beautiful person who owned the glass slipper. So a few days later, the king's son had it proclaimed, by sound of trumpet, that he would marry her whose foot this slipper would just fit. He and his courtiers began to try the slipper on the princesses and the duchesses and all the court, but in vain. Finally, one of the courtiers brought the slipper to the two stepsisters, who did all they possibly could to force their feet into the slipper. But they did not succeed.

Cinderella knew that it was her slipper and said to them, "Let me see if it will fit me." Her sisters burst out laughing and began to banter with her. The gentleman, who had been sent to try the slipper on the young women of the kingdom, looked earnestly at Cinderella, and, finding her to be very beautiful, said that it was only just that she should try it on as well, since he had orders to let everyone try.

He had Cinderella sit down, and when he put the slipper on her foot, he found that it went on very easily, fitting her as if it had been made of wax. Cinderella's two stepsisters were greatly astonished, even more so when Cinderella pulled the other slipper out of her pocket and put it on her other foot. Then the fairy godmother arrived and touched her wand to Cinderella's clothes, making them richer and more magnificent than the ones she had worn before.

Cinderella was taken to the young prince, dressed as she was. He thought she was more charming than before and, a few days after, married her. Cinderella, who was no less good than beautiful, gave her two sisters lodgings in the palace.

Oh, the glass slipper. We all wait for it in one form or another. We sit, sometimes anxiously, sometimes patiently, waiting for that prince to show up and make our lives better. But what you don't know is that the prince is probably waiting for his princess to do the same. How about if everyone makes their own lives better, and then join and magnify the wonder?

If you are waiting for a fairy godmother to assist you, look in the mirror. You have the magic to make your dreams come true. Look to your own talents and to the support of family and friends. But most of all, remember there are no glass slippers.

Many are not born in the best of circumstances. Even good circumstances can turn bad when the players in your environment change. Surviving is all you can do until you find a way out. It is terrifying to be in a circumstance you did not ask for and over which you have no control. But you try to make the best of it and survive.

The best plan is to rise above and beyond the situation, leave what you don't want in the past and to have a good life. But first, you must survive the experiences. You may come out with scars, but repair is at hand. Just survive the best you can, and later you can cleanse yourself of the toxins left by your experience. Don't let bad circumstances or environments turn you into a person you don't want to be. Remember who you are, and you will be rewarded or not for that which you choose to be.

Everyone has breaks—just be prepared to take advantage of them when they happen. There are no fairy godmothers. The magic lies within yourself, in the beauty of who you are and what you will become. Make your own dreams come true.

14

Attain and Maintain

"Nothing great was ever achieved without enthusiasm."
—Ralph Waldo Emerson

Hoping We Have It Now

Fear hinders us. It prevents us from learning from our experiences. We should grow with each day; instead, some of us shrink, withdrawing into nothingness. We may withdraw from life in order to save ourselves from failure. However, this type of choice is failure too, failure to take all we can get from life and to be all we can be. Every experience moves us forward, toward a greater understanding of ourselves—if we use our experiences this way. When we withdraw, we stay stuck in a world we should have left behind.

Yesterday is gone, but its experiences will be reflected in the choices we make today. We can learn from both the good and bad experiences of the past. What we have done today will greatly influence the direction we chose tomorrow. We can't change what has happened, but we can learn from it and move forward.

Our dreams motivate us. We need the courage to move toward them, taking the necessary steps to realize those dreams. We must trust in ourselves and believe we have what it takes.

Goals

Goals are realistically defined dreams. They are dreams that have been spelled out. Goals give direction to our lives. We need to know who we are and where we want to go. The paths we take to those goals offer daily satisfaction, moment by moment. Too often we keep our sights on a goal's completion, rather than on the process toward that goal. We need to appreciate the day-to-day process that makes the completion possible.

Stay Motivated

For those who have had hard lives, it is difficult to get motivated. We can choose to believe we are capable and competent. Or we can choose to believe that we are inadequate.

There are positive thoughts and actions that will keep you motivated.

1. Focus on the positive, but don't ignore the negative.

2. Develop high self-esteem by believing that you have talents and skills.

3. Use positive self-talk and self-thought.

4. Focus on clear, specific goals.

5. Take responsibility for your life.

6. Stay in the present. The past can be an obstacle.

Each of us is unique. There is no one else who can offer the world what each of us can. We often fail to realize our worth. We are needed, and knowing this brings self-satisfaction and happiness.

Focus on successes not failure. You have to have a sense of vision to see what you are capable of achieving. Be realistic with your vision. It helps to realize what paths you should take. Vision gives us hope to strive toward a better life and a better self. We are all we need to be right now, at this very moment.

If you trust that you are all you need to be to reach a goal, it will motivate you. Are you motivated or are you still living in a fantasy world (or should I say nightmare)? You need to trust yourself. You need to

- Set high standards for yourself

- Believe in yourself

- Maintain enthusiasm

- See problems as challenges and opportunities

- Have a positive self-image

Doing these things will keep your motivation alive. Otherwise, you will do just enough to get by, avoiding things and putting them off until you are "in the right mood." Commit yourself to a productive, meaningful life that will contribute to your good and the good of others.

Stay on the Right Path

You'll see many possibilities on the way to a better life. In choosing a path, use a road map that encourages you to choose quality over quantity. If you want to have experiences of quality, you have to give them your full attention. Don't focus on the future, or on what you may have instead of on what you do have, right now. Focusing on the future will cause you to be dissatisfied with the present.

Don't act on impulses; let them pass. You will then become a better judge of which ones are worth acting on. Take time to listen to other people. They may have something to say that may benefit you.

Be patient with yourself, your talents, and the people in your life. You don't have to get everything this very moment, and everything does not have to be perfect. Make sure that what you want will be good for you in the long run.

Monitor your progress and make assessments every step of the way. Ask yourself if you are still on the path you intended. Are you reaching the goals you set for yourself? Asking these questions will help keep you on the right path.

Stay open-minded so that you can learn from the experiences around you. To learn from your experiences, you need to stay open and positive. Sometimes we don't want to hear things that may go against our dreams. See these things as obstacles, not roadblocks. If you ignore the obstacles and don't deal with them, they will come from behind and derail you.

Our wants in life may be simple, or they may be complex. Our wants may confuse us because they don't seem to make the kind of sense we feel they should. Things clear up if we are patient. Too often, we look back on our lives with regret. Let the past go. We have learned lessons from those mistakes, and every day is a new beginning.

Discouraged?

There will be many things that discourage us. There will be many times when we feel we can't go on. It may seem like doors that are open for others are closed to us. You can look at it this way: doors do not close unless a new direction is called for. We must learn to trust that no obstacle is without its purpose, however baffling it may seem. If you are constantly discouraged on a path you have chosen, you may want to step back and reevaluate what you are doing.

- Whatever is occurring in the present is what you need to deal with right now.

- You may need to prioritize your challenges, define the challenges better, or explore different ways to overcome a challenge.

- Stay with the truth. Be willing to be with your whole truth, whatever it is.

- Avoid procrastination. It keeps you from accomplishing what you are able to achieve.

- The more support you have for your personal motivation, the easier it will be for you to achieve both personal and professional goals.

- Most people want to run from challenges. Escaping not only hinders growth but pulls you down.

Meet Challenges with Optimism

We easily forget that our growth comes from the difficult as well as the good times. We develop tools from difficult experiences and can reap benefits from the problems we face. The barriers that get in the way may confuse, frustrate, and even depress us. But we must move forward with persistence and push the barriers aside. You can count on unexpected experiences that will bring moments of joy and sorrow. Life is seldom what we expect. But if we have learned anything from past experiences, we have learned that we will survive. How we survive will depend on us.

Self-esteem and confidence usually develop from having positive experiences. Search out activities and tasks that fit your talents and that give you these positive experiences. Choose tasks that will help you develop into a better person. Doing so will add to your self-esteem.

Avoid negative self-talk that brings up every possible problem you may encounter or have encountered. Be prepared to handle problems but don't dwell on them.

You should always seek the truth no matter how painful it may be. If we observe ourselves, we will see that many explanations we give ourselves for our behavior are excuses that we use to defend ourselves.

Love Thyself

Loving ourselves entails a strong acceptance of who we really are. We have to accept who we are and how our experiences have contributed to who we are. We don't need to accept this as a permanent condition, but it is who we are right now.

Each experience has something to offer. We keep the good that has been given us and resolve the bad so we can discard it. When we settle into ourselves as we actually are, without attempting to change our experience, we will be able to accept the experience but also determine the effect it will have on us.

Loving yourself includes many steps. Most important of these steps is personal development, which is essential if you are to be truthful with yourself. Be honest with yourself and others about your genuine feelings and needs. Resist the temptation to impress others or inflate your importance. You will impress people more deeply by being authentic. Needing to be accepted by others is one of the most negative obstacles to truth. Some people adapt to the expectations of others to the point of losing who they are. Develop yourself by resisting doing what is acceptable just to be accepted. It is important for you to stay true to your own values.

Develop sensitivity in your relationships. Let people know who you really are and where you are coming from. Be honest and forthcoming. Sharing makes others feel that you can be trusted. This does not mean that you have to reveal everything about yourself.

Quiet time is important. Take breaks. You can drive yourself and others to exhaustion pursuing goals relentlessly. You then loose yourself in these goals, letting the goals define who you are.

Each of us should live in good conscience. Life presents us with many opportunities to see our personalities in action and to allow our basic nature to come forth. Let your nature be the best you have to offer.

When faced with adversity, remember the survivors described in this book. When challenges seem too difficult to bring about success, remember that success comes from hard and sometimes painful work. The next time you decide to hide in your fantasies, waiting for a magical cure instead of taking reality by the horns and riding it through, remember there is no glass slipper.

APPENDIX

Evaluations and Assessments

The following are two questionnaires. One will help you evaluate the biographies you have read. The other will help you evaluate yourself. Using these questionnaires will assist you in developing the questions you need to ask in order to identify problematic issues that need resolution, both in the lives of the survivors presented in this book and in your own life. The questionnaires will also assist you in identifying assets and personal strengths that are needed to have a healthy peaceful life.

The first evaluation, the Survivor Assessment Questionnaire, can be used to evaluate the issues and strengths of each survivor. By evaluating the survivors presented in this book, you increase your ability to identify your own issues and strengths.

The second evaluation is the Self-Assessment Questionnaire. When you are ready to evaluative yourself, use this questionnaire. Remember when you are evaluating yourself that you are a survivor, just like the women in this book. Your issues will not be resolved here. But much can be revealed, and you will be on your way to a healthier, happier life.

Survivor Assessment Questionnaire

1. What painful childhood experiences can you identify in each survivor's life?

2. How did each survivor react to these experiences?

3. Were the situations resolved?

4. If so, how were they resolved?

5. If they weren't resolved, how did they affect each survivor's life?

6. Do you see problematic thoughts or behaviors in each survivor's life that may have been caused by unresolved issues?

7. Do you see a pattern of positive or negative thoughts?

8. How did each survivor make her goals realistic and attainable?

9. What did each survivor have to change in her earlier self to accomplish her goals?

10. What were the three most important lessons learned during each survivor's life struggles? List three for each survivor.

Self-Assessment Questionnaire

1.   What painful childhood experiences can you remember?

2.   How did you react to each of these experiences?

3.   Were they resolved?

4.   If they were resolved, how did you resolve them?

5.   If they were not resolved, how might they be affecting your life today?

6.   Can you identify problematic thoughts or behaviors that may have been caused by these unresolved issues?

7.   Do you have frequent negative thoughts? If so, what are they?

8.   How are negative thoughts affecting your outlook on life?

9.   Are you where you want to be in life?

10. What are your goals?

11. Are your goals realistic?

12. What do you need to change in your life, and in yourself, to make your goals attainable?

Main Chapter Highlights

Chapter One: Survive!
Adversities, challenges, being a survivor, coping strategies, painful experiences, motivation, learning from life

Chapter Two: Live!
Keep life simple, decision making, problem solving, identifying emotions, source of emotions, trust, healthy relationships

Chapter Three: The *Hansel and Gretel* Experience

Chapter Four: Barbra Streisand: A Queen in Her Glory
Parental neglect, child neglect, physical and emotional abuse, self-image, body image, goal-setting, persistence

Chapter Six: Oprah Winfrey: Her Highness's Power
Abandonment, maternal neglect, sexual abuse, incest, juvenile disobedience, identifying your strengths, using your assets, parental guidance

Chapter Seven: Falling with *Alice in Wonderland*

Chapter Eight: Drew Barrymore: A Popular Princess
Physical abuse, emotional abuse, substance abuse, peer pressure, abandonment, breaking dysfunctional family cycles, belonging

Chapter Nine: Waking Up with *Sleeping Beauty*

Chapter Ten: Halle Berry: Royal Beauty
Identity, self esteem, domestic abuse, relationships, codependency, discrimination, maternal readiness, independence

Chapter Eleven: Enlightenment from *The Wizard of Oz*

Chapter Twelve: Demi Moore: A Duchess's Determination
Domestic abuse, parental alcohol abuse, substance abuse, self esteem, body image, security, acceptance, parent-child roles

Chapter Thirteen: The Glass Slipper: *Cinderella's Lessons*

Chapter Fourteen: Attain and Maintain
Positive thoughts, habits and skills for success, commitment, responsibility, goal setting, balancing your goals, monitoring and maintaining progress

Bibliography for individual quotes

Chapter Four: Barbra Streisand, Taught the Hard Way

"Myths are a waste of time. They prevent progression." Streisand, Barbra. http://www.Thinkexist.com (accessed November 14, 2005)

"To have ego means to believe in your own strength. And to also be open to other people's views. It is to be open, not closed. My ego is responsible for my doing what I do—bad or good." Streisand, Barbra. http://www.Thinkexist.com (accessed November 14, 2005)

"I just don't want to be hampered by my own limitations." Streisand, Barbra. http://www.brainyquote.com (accessed November 14, 2005)

"I am simple, complex, generous, selfish, unattractive, beautiful, lazy, and driven." Streisand, Barbra. http://www.brainyquote.com (accessed November 14, 2005)

"You have got to discover you, what you do, and trust it." Streisand, Barbra. http://www.quotationspage.com (accessed November 14, 2005)

"I'm not that ambitious any more. I just like my privacy. I wish I really wasn't talked about at all." Streisand, Barbra. http://www.brainyquote.com (accessed November 14, 2005)

"Why is it men are permitted to be obsessed about their work, but women are only permitted to be obsessed about men?" Streisand, Barbra. http://www.brainyquote.com (accessed November 14, 2005)

"A human being is only interesting if he's in contact with himself." Streisand, Barbra. http://www.quotationspage.com (accessed November 14, 2005)

"I learned you have to trust yourself, be what you are, and do what you ought to do the way you should do it." Streisand, Barbra. http://www.quotationspage.com (accessed November 14, 2005)

Chapter Six: Oprah Winfrey: Trial by Fire

"It doesn't matter who you are, where you come from. The ability to triumph begins with you. Always." (O, The Oprah Magazine. New York, NY: Hearst Communications)

"Lots of people want to ride with you in the limo, but what you want is someone who will take the bus with you when the limo breaks down." (O, The Oprah Magazine. New York, NY: Hearst Communications)

"I have a lot of things to prove to myself. One is that I can live my life fearlessly." (O, The Oprah Magazine. New York, NY: Hearst Communications)

"Your true passion should feel like breathing; it's that natural." (O, The Oprah Magazine. New York, NY: Hearst Communications)

"My philosophy is that not only are you responsible for your life, but doing the best at this moment puts you in the best place for the next moment." (O, The Oprah Magazine. New York, NY: Hearst Communications)

"Become the change you want to see—those are words I live by." (O, The Oprah Magazine. New York, NY: Hearst Communications)

"Cheers to a new year and another chance for us to get it right." (O, The Oprah Magazine. New York, NY: Hearst Communications)

"I define joy as a sustained sense of well-being and internal peace—a connection to what matters." (O, The Oprah Magazine. New York, NY: Hearst Communications)

"I know for sure that what we dwell on is who we become." (O, The Oprah Magazine. New York, NY: Hearst Communications)

"I trust that everything happens for a reason, even when we're not wise enough to see it." (O, The Oprah Magazine. New York, NY: Hearst Communications)

"If you want your life to be more rewarding, you have to change the way you think." (O, The Oprah Magazine. New York, NY: Hearst Communications)

"Understand that the right to choose your own path is a sacred privilege. Use it. Dwell in possibility." (O, The Oprah Magazine. New York, NY: Hearst Communications)

"We are each responsible for our own life—no other person is or even can be." (O, The Oprah Magazine. New York, NY: Hearst Communications)

"Whatever you fear most has no power—it is your fear that has the power." (O, The Oprah Magazine. New York, NY: Hearst Communications)

"Energy is the essence of life. Every day you decide how you're going to use it by knowing what you want and what it takes to reach that goal, and by maintaining focus." (O, The Oprah Magazine. New York, NY: Hearst Communications)

"Most all the mistakes I've made in my life, I've made because I was trying to please other people." (O, The Oprah Magazine. New York, NY: Hearst Communications)

Chapter Eight: Drew Barrymore, Mom Never Taught Me This

"It's only through listening that you learn, and I never want to stop learning." Barrymore, Drew. http://www.Thinkexist.com (accessed November 14, 2005)

"I believe that everything happens for a reason, but I think it's important to seek out that reason—that's how we learn." Barrymore, Drew. http://www.Brainyquote.com (accessed November 14, 2005)

"I don't know anybody's road that's been paved perfectly for them, there are no manuals, you don't know what life has in store for you." Barrymore, Drew. http://www.Brainyquote.com (accessed November 14, 2005)

"My whole life, I've wanted to feel comfortable in my skin. It's the most liberating thing in the world." Barrymore, Drew. http://www.Brainyquote.com (accessed November 14, 2005)

"If you're going to be alive and on this planet, you have to, like, suck the marrow out of every day and get the most out of it." Barrymore, Drew. http://www.Thinkexist.com (accessed November 14, 2005)

"And when things come clear to you, no matter how you had to get there, as long as you come out the other side of it, then it's all worth it." Barrymore, Drew. (Geocites)

We've got to learn hard things in our lifetime, but it's love that gives you the strength. It's being nice to people and having a lot of fun and laughing harder than anything, hopefully every single day of your life. Barrymore, Drew. http://www.Allmyquotes.com (accessed November 15, 2005)

"You've just got to do the best that you can." Barrymore, Drew. http://www.Brainyquote.com (accessed November 14, 2005)

"I have no regrets. Everything you've been through makes you what you are." Barrymore, Drew. http://www.Brainyquote.com (accessed November 14, 2005)

"If you're going to go through hell…I suggest you come back learning something." Barrymore, Drew. http://www.Brainyquote.com (accessed November 14, 2005)

Life is very interesting…in the end, some of your greatest pains, become your greatest strengths. Barrymore, Drew. http://www.Allmyquotes.com (accessed November 15, 2005)

Chapter Ten: Halle Berry, Reality Testing

Being thought of as "a beautiful woman" has spared me nothing in life. No heartache, no trouble. Beauty is essentially meaningless. Berry, Halle. http://www.Allmyquotes.com (accessed November 15, 2005)

"I respond well to tortured characters. There's a place in me that can really relate to being the underdog." Berry, Halle. http://www.Pulseweekly.com (accessed November 15, 2005)

"I think it's always best to be who you are." Berry, Halle. http://www.Thinkexist.com (accessed November 14, 2005)

"I know that there is a God—the God within me that's always present and will protect me." Berry, Halle. http://www.Thinkexist.com (accessed November 14, 2005)

"I'm not afraid to climb any mountain, because I know that I'm protected. Even if I fall and die, I'm still protected. My faith is on that level."http://www. Allgreatquotes.com (accessed November 15, 2005)

"I'm still a work in progress, but I know that as long as I stay close to God I'll be all right." Berry, Halle. http://www.Thinkexist.com (accessed November 14, 2005)

"I understand now that 'special love' exists between two people when the passions lie beneath the surface." Berry, Halle. http://www.Thinkexist.com (accessed November 14, 2005)

There's a place in me that can really relate to being the underdog. I'm always fighting to overcome the obstacle. I can really understand what's that about. Berry, Halle. http://www.quotemonk.com (accessed November 15, 2005)

I'm really comfortable with who I am now, and not so much in need of the approval of other people like I used to be, and so I'm learning to look the other way. (King,2002)

I think sometimes it's hard for people to see past the physical. But honestly I could think of worst problems to have. I think it's harder being a black woman in this industry than looking the way I do. Yes, I think it's harder being a black woman than being considered beautiful. (King,2002)

Chapter Twelve: Demi Moore, A Twisty Winding Road

It's how we choose to deal with those things that happen in our lives that matters. Moore, Demi. (Hal Rubenstein,1996)

"Marriage was a goal. A family, for me as a young girl, was my image of what I hoped for. It was part of the big picture." Moore, Demi. http://www. Brainyquote.com (accessed November 14, 2005)

"The truth is you can have a great marriage, but there are still no guarantees."
Moore, Demi. http://www.Brainyquote.com (accessed November 14, 2005)

Success has to be an inside job. Happiness does not come from external material
things. Even people don't make us ultimately happy. Moore, Demi. (Hal Rubenstein, 1996)

"I want things to be the best they can be. I want greatness." Moore, Demi.
http://www.Thinkexist.com (accessed November 14, 2005)

"I don't think I plan that far in advance. I try to focus on the present, what I'm
doing now. Moore, Demi. (Hal Rubenstein, 1996)

I feel like the best design I can have is an awareness of where I've come from so
that I don't repeat myself. Moore, Demi. (Hal Rubenstein, 1996)

"Happiness does not come from external material things. Even people don't
make us ultimately happy." Moore, Demi. http://www.Brainyquote.com
(accessed November 14, 2005)
(Brainyquote)

Well, like many people, I think I'm my own worst critic. And I think I take a lot
out in an internally abusive way, looking at how I measure up, which usually was
never enough. I never, never was as good as someone else. Moore, Demi. (Hal
Rubenstein, 1996)

Bibliography

Aber, L., J. Allen, V. Carlson, and D. Cicchetti. "The Effects of Maltreatment on Development During Early Childhood. Recent Studies and Their Theoretical, Clinical, and Policy Implications. In *Child Maltreatment: Theory and Research on the Causes and Consequences of Child Abuse and Neglect*. Ed. Dante Cucchetti & Vicki Carlson. New York: Cambridge University Press, 1989.

Amber, Jeannie. January 1, 1997. "Young and Abused: Any Young Woman Can Fall Prey to an Abusive, Violent Man, No Matter How Smart or How Self-Confident She Is." *Essence*. .

Aronson, Virginia. *Drew Barrymore: Overcoming Adversity.* Broomall, PA.:Chelsea House Publications, 1999.

Austin, Nancy. "The Power of the Pyramid: The Foundation of Human Psychology and, Thereby, of Motivation, Maslow's Hierarchy Is One Powerful Pyramid." *Incentive*, July 1, 2002.

Barrymore, Drew. *Little Girl Lost.* Reissue edition. New York, NY: Pocket, 1991.

Bass, Ellen and Laura Davis. *The Courage to Heal. A Guide for Woman Survivors of Child Sexual Abuse.* Third edition. np: Perennial, 1994.

Beitchman, J., K. Zucker, J. Hood, G. daCosta, D. Akman, and E. Cassavia. 1992. "A Review of the Long-term Effects of Child Sexual Abuse." *Child Abuse and Neglect*.

Berry, Halle. CNN Larry King Live. "Interview with Pierce Brosnan", Halle Berry. Interviewed by Larry King. November 7, 2002.

Bradshaw, John. *Healing the Shame That Binds You.* Deerfield Beach, FL: Health Communications Inc., 1998.

Brown, Wall. *Emotional Abuse and Neglect of Children*. New York, NY: William Galdden Foundation, 1990.

Buffington, Sherry. *Who's Got the Compass? I Think I'm Lost: A Guide to Finding Your Ideal Self*. np: Bookpartners, 1998.

Burney, Robert. *Codependence: The Dance of Wounded Souls*. Cambria, CA: Joy to You and Me Enterprises; 1st Edition, 1995.

Cerel J., M. A. Fristad, E. B. Weller, and R. A. Weller. 1999. "Suicide-bereaved Children and Adolescents: A Controlled Longitudinal Examination." *Journal of the American Academy of Child and Adolescent Psychiatry* 38: 672-679.

Chase, Kenneth A. 2003. "Factors Associated with Partner Violence among Female Alcoholic Patients and Their Male Partners." *Journal of Studies on Alcohol*.

Treanor, Veronica. 1989. "Children of Alcoholics." *Pediatrics for Parents*.

Corbett, Coryanne. June 1, 1995. "The Winner Within: A Hands-on Guide to Healthy Self Esteem." *Essence*.

Crespi, Tony. 1997. "Children of Alcoholics and Adolescence: Individuation, Development, and Family Systems." *Adolescence*.

Crespi, Tony and J. P. Fieldman. 2002. "Child Sexual Abuse: Offenders, Disclosure, and School-Based Initiatives." *Adolescence*.

David, Rebecca. Demi Moore. http://. about.com. Demi Moore. (accessed November 14, 2005.

Dear, Greg & Claire Roberts. 2002 "Relationships between Codependency and Femininity and Masculinity." *Sex Roles: A Journal of Research*.

Denton, Rhonda. 1994. "The Relationship between Family Variables and Adolescent Substance Abuse: A Literature Review." Adolescence, Summer 1994.

Domestic Violence—A Guide for Health Care Professionals. State of New Jersey. Department of Community Affairs, 1990.

Drew, Rachel Arnold. 2003. "Out of the Darkened Room: When a Parent is Depressed: Protecting the Children and Strengthening the Family." *Journal of the American Academy of Child and Adolescent Psychiatry.*

Emshoff, James G. 1999. "Prevention and Intervention Strategies with Children of Alcoholics." *Pediatrics.*

Farley, Christopher John. *Introducing Halle Berry.*New York, NY: Pocket, 2002.

Gallant, William. 1998. "The Association of Personality Characteristics with Parenting Problems among Alcoholic Couples." *American Journal of Drug and Alcohol Abuse.*

Garson, Helen. *Oprah Winfrey: A Biography.* Westport, CT: Greenwood Biographies, 2004.

Geffner, Robert and Carol Mantooth. Ending Spouse/Partner Abuse: A Psychoeducational Approach for Individuals & Couples. New York, NY. Springer Publishing Company, 2000. 2003.

Gilbert, Alexander. 2003. "Evolution, Social Roles and the Difference in Shame and Guilt." *Social Research.*

Goodall, Nigel. *Demi Moore: The Most Powerful Women in Hollywood.* N. Pomfrett, VT: Trafalgar Square Books, 2000.

Groves, B., B. Zuckerman, and S. Marans. 1993. "Silent Victims: Children Who Witness Violence." *Journal of the American Medical Association.*

Gunyes, Virginia. April 1993. "Momie Barest:Demi Moore's Mom—Nude!" *High Society.*

Hall, Sarah. "Halle Berry's Stalker Scare". E! News Online. http://eonline.com. (accessed April 26, 2006).

Hamberger, L., Kevin Renzetti, and Claire Renzetti. *Domestic Partner Abuse.* First edition. New York, NY: Springer Publishing Company, 1996.

Hart, Louise. March 22, 1989. "Self-esteem: The Best Gift You Can Give Your Child—and Yourself." *Mothering.*

Hill, Anne E. *Drew Barrymore: People in the News.* San Diego, CA: Lucent Books, 2001.

Hoffman, Bob. *The Negative Love Syndrome.* Rev. edition. South Yarra, Australia: Hoffman Centre, 2000.

Hunt, Majorie. 1997. "A Comparison of Family of Origin Factors between Children of Alcoholics and Children of Non-Alcoholics in a Longitudinal Pane." *American Journal of Drug and Alcohol Abuse.*

Hussong, Andrea. 1998. "Pathways of Risk for Accelerated Heavy Alcohol Use among Adolescent Children of Alcoholic Parents." *Journal of Abnormal Child Psychology.*

"Improve Your Self-esteem for a Healthier You." May 10, 2004. *Jet.*

Inglis, Ruth and P. Owens. *Sins of the Father: A Study of the Physical and Emotional Abuse of Children.* First edition. np: 1978.

Jacobson, Neil. March 1, 1998. "Anatomy of a Violent Relationship." *Psychology Today.*

Jaffe, Steven. 1999. "Adolescent Substance Abuse: Assessment and Treatment." *Adolescent Psychiatry.*

Jakes, T. D. February 1, 2003. "No Man Can Make You Happy." *Essence.*

Johnson, Jeannette. 1999. "Children of Substance Abusers: Overview of Research Findings." *Pediatrics.*

Johnson, Marilyn. September 1997. "Oprah Winfrey: A Life in Books." *Life.*

Kaplan, Sandra, J. Pelcovitz, and David Abruna. 1999. "Child and Adolescent Abuse and Neglect Research: A Review of the Past 10 Years. Part I: Physical and Emotional Abuse and Neglect." *Journal of the Academy of Child and Adolescent Psychiatry.*

Kendall-Tackett, K., L. M. Williams, and D. Finkelhor. 1993. "Impact of Sexual Abuse on Children: A Review and Synthesis of Recent Empirical Studies." *Psychological Bulletin* 113.

Kenyatta, Kelly. *Red Hot Halle: The Story of an American Best Actress.* np: W. H. Publications, 2002.

King, Norman. *Everybody Loves Oprah.* New York: Morrow, 1987.

Klausner, Mary Anne and Bobbie Hasselbring. *Aching for Love.* np: HarperCollins, 1990.

Landon Jr., E. Lard. 1974. "Self Concept, Ideal Self Concept and Consumer Purchase Intentions." *Journal of Consumer Research: An Interdisciplinary Quarterly* 1, no. 2.

Lang, Alan, R. 1999. "Effects of Alcohol Intoxication on Parenting Behavior in Interactions with Child Confederates Exhibiting Normal or Deviant Behaviors." *Journal of Abnormal Child Psychology.*

Langer, Ellen. November 1, 1999. "Self-esteem vs. Self-respect. The Power Lies in the Difference." *Psychology Today.*

Lapchick, Richard. July 4, 1994. "We Can't Overlook the Ugliness Any Longer." *Sporting News.*

Lease, Suzanne H. 2002. "A Model of Depression in Adult Children of Alcoholics and Nonalcoholics." *Journal of Counseling and Development.*

Lewis, Michael. 2003. "The Role of the Self in Shame." *Social Research.*

Lewis, Thomas, Fari Aminin, and Richard Lannon. *A General Theory of Love.* np: Random House, 2000.

Lowe, Jane. *Oprah Winfrey Speaks: Insights from the World's Most Influential Voice.* np: Wiley, 1998.

Mair, George. *Oprah Winfrey: The Real Story.* np: Carol Publishing Corp., 1994.

Martin, James. 1995. "Intimacy, Loneliness, and Openness to Feelings in Adult Children of Alcoholics." *Health and Social Work.*

Maslow, Abraham. "Conflict, Frustration and the Theory of Threat." *Journal of Abnormal and Social Psychology* 38.

Maslow, Abraham . 1943. "The Authoritarian Character Study." *Journal of Social Psychology* 18:401-411.

Maslow, Abraham .1943. "The Theory of Human Motivation." *Psychological Review* 50:360-396.

Mayer, Larry. *Oprah Winfrey: The Soul and Spirit of a Superstar.* Chicago, IL: Triumph Books, 2000.

McIntosh, Sarah. Oprah Winfrey: *Talk Show Legend* (African American Biographies). Berkley Heights, NJ: Enslow, 1999.

McKay, James. 1992. "The Relationship of Pretreatment Family Functioning to Drinking Behavior during Follow-up by Alcoholic Parents." *American Journal of Drug and Alcohol Abuse.*

McKay, Matthew and Patrick Fanning. *Self-Esteem: A Proven Program of Cognitive Techniques for Assessing, Improving, and Maintaining Your Self-Esteem.* Third edition. np: New Harbinger Publications, 2000.

McNeal, C. and P. R. Amato. 1998. "Individuals Exposed to Domestic Violence in Childhood often Report Adjustment Difficulties in Early Adulthood. Parents' Marital Violence: Long-term Consequences for Children." *Journal of Family Issues.*

Miller, Susan. *But Mom, I Didn't Want to Move: Easing the Impact of Moving on Your Children*. np: Focus on the Family Publishing, 2004.

Mintle, Linda. *Breaking Free From a Negative Self-Image*. np: Charisma House, 2002.

Psychology Today Staff. "Mired in Misery—Self-esteem Problems." July 1, 1992. *Psychology Today*.

Moore, Demi. Interview by Hal Rubenstein. July 1996. Brant Publications, Inc. Gale Group, 2000.

Mosteller, Rolland. *The Abusive Personality: Violence and Control in Intimate Relationships*. New York: Guilford Press. 2000.

"Moving and Behavior—Relocation." 1993. *Pediatrics for Parents*.

"Moving: Problems when Kids Object." April 1, 1993. *USA Today*.

MSN Movies Entertainment: Celebrity Information Demi Moore. www.msn.com.

Ness D. and C. R. Pfeffer. 1990. "Sequelae for Bereavement Resulting from Suicide." *American Journal of Psychiatry* 147(3):279-85.

O'Brien, Daniel. *Halle Berry*. Littleton, CO: Reynolds & Hearn LTD, 2003.

Olkowski, Thomas T. and Lynn Parker. *Moving With Children: A Parent's Guide*. Surrey, UK: Gylantic Publishing, 1993.

Oprah Winfrey.Academy of Achievement. The Hall of Business. Chicago, Illinois. Interview by Academy of Achievement staff. February 21, 1991.

Orie, Kathleen. 1998. "Screening Men for Partner Violence in a Primary Care Setting: A New Strategy for Detecting Domestic Violence." *Journal of Family Practice*.

Palmer, Nancie. 1997. "Resilience in Adult Children of Alcoholics: A Nonpathological Approach to Social Work Practice." *Health and Social Work.*

Pelham, William. 1997. "Effects of Deviant Child Behavior on Parental Distress and Alcohol Consumption in Laboratory Interactions." *Journal of Abnormal Child Psychology.*

Randolph, Laura. August 1999. "Halle Berry" *Ebony Magazine.*

Reise, Randall. *Her Name is Barbra: An Intimate Portrait of the Real Barbra Streisand.* np: Carol Publishing, 1993.

Renn, Dory. 2000. "Emotional Abuse of the Child." *Adolescence.*

Rowe, Cynthia. 2003. "Substance Abuse." *Journal of Marital and Family Therapy.*

Sanello, Frank. *Halle Berry: A Life Story.* np: Virgin Books, 2003.

Schwartz, Sandra. 1994. "Feel Good about Your Diabetes and Self-esteem." *Diabetes Forecast.*

Scott, Teresa and Caine Loring. 1997. "Codependency: An Interpersonal Phenomenon." *Sex Roles: A Journal of Research.*

Caine, Teresa. 1995 "Secret to Serenity: Understanding Codependency." *Vibrant Life.*

Smullens, SaraKay. 2002. "The 5 Cycles of Emotional Abuse: Investigating a Malignant Victimization." *Annals of the American Psychotherapy Association.*

Spaccarelli, S. 1994. "Stress, Appraisal, and Coping in Child Sexual Abuse: A Theoretical and Empirical Review." *Psychological Bulletin* 116(2)340-362.

Spada, James. *Streisand: Her Life.* First edition. New York, NY: Crown, 1995.

Stark, Elizabeth. January 1, 1987. "Forgotten Victims: Children of Alcoholics." *Psychology Today.*

Starr, R. H. and D. A. Wolfe, eds. *The Effects of Child Abuse and Neglect: Issues and Research*. New York: Guildford, 1991.

Sutherland, Bryony and Lucy Ellis. *Drew Barrymore: The Biography*. London, UK: Aurum Press, 2003.

Tangney, Price and Rhonda L. Dearing. *Shame and Guilt (Emotions and Social Behavior)*. New York: Guildford, 2003.

Tatlor, Susan. September 1, 1994. "Owning Your Life—Women and Domestic Violence (editorial)." *Essence*.

Tomori, Martina. 1994. "Personality Characteristics of Adolescents with Alcoholic Parents." *Adolescence*.

Touri. January 20, 2001. "Portrait of a Lady" *USA Weekend*.

Trickett, P. K. and F. W. Putman. 1993. "Impact of Child Sexual Abuse on Females: Toward a Developmental, Psychobiological Integration." *Psychological Science* 4 (: pages).

Van Dongen, Carol. 1991. "Experiences of Family Members after a Suicide. *Journal of Family Practice*.

Wade, Brenda. April 1, 1996. "Fear of Abandonment: A Psychologist Helps Us Heal Hidden Wounds that Hold Us Back." *Essence*.

Washington, Elsie & Joy Duckett Cain. August 1, 1996. "Words that Wound—Self-esteem" *Parenting Guide*. Essence.

"Why Do Women Tolerate Domestic Violence?" September 22, 1997. *Jet*.

Winfrey, Oprah. Commencement Address. May 30, 1997. Wellesley College, Wellesley, MS.

Winfrey, Oprah and Bill Adler. *The Uncommon Wisdom of Oprah Winfrey: A Portrait in Her Own Words*. New York, NY: Birch Lane Press, 1997.

Wolfe, D. A., R. J. McMahon, and R. D. Peters, eds. *Child Abuse: New Directions in Prevention and Treatment across the Lifespan.* Thousand Oaks, CA: Sage, 1997.

Wolichick, Sharlene. 2002. "Fear of Abandonment as a Mediator of the Relations between Divorce Stressors and Mother-Child Relationship Quality and Children's Adjustment Problems." *Journal of Child Abnormal Psychology.*

"Your Secret Mood Booster." September 1, 1999. *Psychology Today.*

Zannos, Susan. *Drew Barrymore: Real-Life Reader Biography.* Hockessin, DE: Mitchell Lane Publishers, 2000.

Zec, Donald. *Barbra: A Biography of Barbra Streisand.* New York, NY: St. Martins Press, 1982.

About the Author

Dr. Coffey is a Clinical Psychologist. She has an extensive history as a therapist who conducts individual and group sessions as a therapist in community mental health programs with clients who suffer from issues addressed in *No Glass Slipper*.

In her private practice as a Clinical Forensic Psychologist she is considered an expert in her field. She specializes in clinical diagnosis, prognosis, and treatment recommendations for individuals with legal difficulties which may have a clinical basis rooted in past traumatic unresolved experiences. As a psychotherapist, she conducts group and individual therapy, which includes writing and developing materials for group and individual sessions, evaluations, and training.

In addition to her private practice she has treated families and couples, assisting with building stronger healthier bonds in their relationships. She has practiced in semi-hospitalization programs addressing severe depression, anxiety and other debilitating mental illnesses which required extensive treatment and has worked in a day treatment program providing continuous group support and psycho-educational programs. Dr Coffey also has experience as a clinician working with individuals who are in need of both substance and mental health treatment.

In her years as a mental health clinician she has evaluated and diagnosed a wide range of symptoms which iclude clients needing answers and assistance with unhealthy thought and behavior patterns which have developed throughout their lives. Her years of experience has given her the opportunity to develop, test, and refine the use of survivor biographies as a therapeutic tool which has proven to be successful with her clients who have had traumatic experiences which are unresolved.

Dr. Coffey believes that not only do you learn from your experiences but can learn from the experiences of others. In her group sessions her clients share their experiences and lessons and thrive. She uses comments from clients who have used her materials to further develop her therapeutic tools with the goal of delivering quality guidance with or without the assistance of a therapist.

Dr. Coffey has a Bachelors degree in developmental and social psychology from the University of Southern California, a Masters degree in social psychology from California State University, Los Angeles, and a Doctorate degree in clinical psychology from Southern California University. She is a licensed therapist in Virginia and Washington D.C.and was granted diplomat status in psychotherapy due to her extensive education, training, and experience. She is a Master Addictions Counselor and a Certified Criminal Justice Specialist. Time and time again she has been certified as an expert in her field in court because of her ability to relate past experiences with present behavior and thought processes.

978-0-595-38603-1
0-595-38603-2

CPSIA information can be obtained at www.ICGtesting.com
Printed in the USA
LVOW12s1807090914

403240LV00002B/382/P